WOMEN
AND
SOMETIMES
MEN

❀ *Florida Scott-Maxwell* ❀

WOMEN
AND
SOMETIMES
MEN

Alfred A. Knopf New York

1957

L.C. catalog card number: 57–9128

© *Florida Scott-Maxwell, 1957*

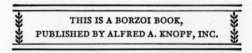

THIS IS A BORZOI BOOK,
PUBLISHED BY ALFRED A. KNOPF, INC.

FIRST AMERICAN EDITION

"The modern woman stands before a great cultural task which means, perhaps, the beginning of a new era."

c. g. jung: *Women in Europe,* 1927

LIONEL TRILLING in his introduction to *The Bostonians* quotes Henry James writing of the death of his mother: "She was our life, she was the house, she was the keystone of the arch. . . . She was patience, she was wisdom, she was exquisite maternity." Then Trilling adds: "His mother was the strength that is not power, as the world knows power, the strength of conservation, the unseen, unregarded, seemingly unexerted force that holds things to their center; she had lived the ancient elemental course of life which is without theory or formulation, too certain of itself and too much at one with itself even to aspire."

I wish to make full acknowledgment to Dr. C. G. Jung, whose concepts I have used, but I must take full responsibility for the many places where I have had only my own experience and that of other women to guide me.

❁ *Contents* ❁

WOMEN

AND

SOMETIMES

MEN

I

We Are Baffled

WOMEN are a subject frequently discussed, never resolved, and they are apt to inflame tempers. Everyone apparently has an idea of what a woman ought to be, and no one seems wholly satisfied with the way she fulfills her role. From the irritation she arouses it almost looks as though she is wanted to change and to improve.

Men often project their own feminine nature onto her, and calling that woman, rail against it; or they may assume that she should remain within the formula of the kind of woman they like, and feel outraged that she is so often outside it. The difficulty is perhaps a matter of definitions, few seeming to fit, and many never worn; until the faults of woman seem so prominent that it is clear many want her to be more likeable as well as more admirable. When a man and a woman discuss this subject they can quickly reach confusion, and the woman may become distraught; for the man talks of the role he expects

[3]

a woman to fulfill, while the woman tries to describe the individual she feels she is, or would be if allowed to discover its confines for herself.

It sometimes looks as though woman would not be woman unless man insisted upon it, since she tends so markedly to be just a human being when away from men, and only on their approach does she begin to play her required role. Which may be the reason why she is so often the actress she is accused of being.

Many men refuse to think about this stormy subject, convinced that it is one of the incurable difficulties of life, and this is disturbingly like saying that woman is incurable. But incurable of what? It is often said that she is less of a problem when she loves and is loved. That is the great solution admittedly, but most women would say that even this enhancing state still leaves her a great deal of herself to be dealt with as best she may. When she loves, and is found lovable, she may care more than ever before who and what she is, in case love should leave her, leaving her much reduced in value. Love is the solution to the problem of women, but love is also the center of her problem. Many men as well as women have loved, but few would say that it ended all difficulties.

Woman has always been the secret side of life, representing the deep feeling that lies between two people. So how can she be fully discussed when the essential things are left unsaid? They are intangible things almost impossible to state, differing between every two people, and even differing frequently between the same two people. These secrecies of living are woman's richness of experience; yet there is a certain danger in standing for the unexplored, since it may also be the neglected or even the dishonored. If the last is so then it must also mean that the feeling life of the man is dishonored, since if you want to judge a man, you must include the women about him in order to come to a true total. Woman herself apparently feels that she has been private too long and now needs the objectivity of publicity.

Women have old reasons for being acutely sensitive about themselves, wincing at any sentence that begins with the word "women." They dread being told once more what a woman is, or should be, and are easily made angry that it is seldom left to women themselves to decide what they rightly are. There is an increasing impatience with old precepts, for some new life is mounting in women. One could almost say that many women are preparing a new birth, and this time it is themselves that stirs within them. So they do not want anyone to tell them what a woman is, for that is what they are discovering for themselves, and sometimes they do it by going down strange paths.

But women are caught, and they are baffled, by the fact that they either live with men, adapting to them as women, as the kind of woman their kind of man likes, or else—to their dismay—they find that when they do not live with a man, but live for their work, doing a man's work, they tend to become almost men themselves. It is this baffling cleft in which many women struggle at the moment.

Just as they gain many new things, as they seem to be

gaining themselves, they find that they are in acute danger of losing themselves. It is so maddening a plight that they are tempted to ignore the entire matter. They often insist that there is nothing further to be said about woman. She is now free, and she is no longer a subject for discussion. Many seem to feel that if women continue to compete with men all will soon be well. But clearly there are many new things to be said about woman. There has seldom been a period when there was so much to say; such novel things, and so far-reaching, extending into every aspect of society. Woman has always had a quality that enables her to become again and again "the new woman," and she has hardly ever been as new as now.

Yet though the subject has to be approached warily, to avoid irritation, remembering that woman is the side of life that is lived, not voiced, felt but not thought, it is still true that she is half the human race, now rising into great prominence, undergoing a striking change, and warranting our most serious attention.

Woman used to stand for relationship, but this is no longer true to the same degree, or in the same way. We only have to consider the number of divorces that take place to see that she refuses relationship for varying reasons, and also in varying ways. Sometimes because she does not like the responsibilities of marriage, and sometimes because she will not endure the terms. Sometimes because she has a high ideal of relationship, and she cannot love where she feels no respect. Perhaps it is here that love should turn into mercy, for this is what many men ask women to do with their love, but it could be here that many women feel too much is asked of them in relationship.

Divorce is so frequent, and so ugly in its findings, that disapproval is natural, but it is part of woman's new freedom, and the place where she steps outside old definitions. She can now refuse to give her body, and this is a new thing for woman: if her marriage ends she can now support herself and retain possession of herself, and this has its own honor. She can be criticized for what she sometimes makes of marriage, but we must remember that when she ends marriage, it may be because the quality of the relation is for her the sacrament. So women represent a new basis of judgment, not that of law but of feeling. This change is far-reaching, of great meaning but with obvious dangers.

Woman's new strength seems to have created a belief in assessing living value; but perhaps we should say that her independence has come at the same time as a general belief in the necessity of measuring not by laws, but by the goodness and badness in the quality of life as it is lived.

Almost all modern women want a more conscious relation with the man than he understands or has time for. Sometimes when a woman seems to a man to be at her most difficult, she is fighting for their relationship. When she is impelled to say: "I exist apart from you, and I will not just be the manager of your private life. Something in me is outraged unless there is a relationship between us that is the cause of our being together." When this is said it can be more constructive than it sounds.

If women are less identified with their homes than they used to be and have other interests than their devotion to the family, it is partly because it is so difficult to establish between the man and the woman the kind of awareness that makes the work of the home, the minutia and the repetition, endurable. When a woman finds that she can do work of recognized value outside her home, it is refreshing and restful to be judged by her work, and not by the very personal opinion of one person. Here she does indeed escape from her old role, and no wonder men feel some disquietude.

Less and less often is modern woman passive, the creator of quiet. Perhaps she never was as passive as men told her it was her true nature to be. But now she makes little pretense of passivity, and when all her energy is needed, and demanded, her inherent passivity is seldom mentioned. Instead she has become terrifyingly active, more active than her husband, and it is often he who helps her, instead of the old way when she helped and rested him.

Our modern pattern of living as well as the financial stress of the times have made it usual for most women to work before marriage, thus gaining independence—long-coveted independence—before entering into the partnership of marriage. Before a woman is a wife she has tasted the keen flavor of impersonal achievement and has become accustomed to the hard give and take of the outside world.

This wide, almost unstateable change, makes marriage very different and it makes a woman a different person to marry. Having worked before marriage, she often continues her work after marriage, and this means that she is not dependent on her husband. No matter what the conveniences of a double income may be it creates a new situation for both.

Money gives the power to act independently, so women now have what they have long lacked, and that is the satisfaction and self-respect of paying for their choice and their decisions, as well as for their mistakes. Men often argue that women like being financially dependent on the man they love, saying it is a true part of oneness, but many women dislike it and even find it humiliating.

Yet being independent is perilously near to being unloving, if we look at marriage through old-fashioned glasses, which we often find we are wearing, or our husbands are wearing. For when a woman earns money she can disagree with her husband, and pay for her disagreement. She no longer coaxes, and he no longer has the final word. This displaces the husband from his old position of authority, and the change is almost greater for him than for her. It gives her self-respect, but it can hurt his pride. He may need this pride, and if robbed of it, he is faced with making a new kind of relationship with his wife. This may be a creative step for him, but it can be a hard one, entailing much generosity, and what amounts to a new concept of marriage and to a new definition of women. So a creative change is taking place in the feminine side of man.

A wife can feel that she ought to agree with her husband, that it distresses him if she doesn't, and she has generations of women behind her who had to agree, and who did it both from duty and from love. If the wife can pay for the things she wants but he does not, it marks their difference. Money being the measure of reality it often is, it shows that they are two people, not one, which can make money say a new truth, and deny an old one. It shows that love once meant that a loving woman always agreed with her husband, that love meant a single vision for two, and that it must in fact have meant much pretense and much conflict.

We hear so much about the new type of woman, the woman who works after marriage, but we hear very little about those quiet, reserved people—husbands who never say anything about the inherent difficulty of being husbands, and who are silent as to what they feel about wives who can stand on their own feet. Many wives are not wives in the old sense. Indeed the old sense has greatly gone; and having gone for many, it affects to some extent those who still live in the old way. The new sense is not wholly declared or clear, and it is naturally very varied. One sees husbands and wives who are a pair of able partners, even brilliant partners whose relationship is almost a public performance, with privacy replaced by extreme frankness before others, and with friends often used as audience for an exhibition of verbal hard hitting. One sees other couples living comfortably in the Stone Age. And all the ages between then and now are well represented.

Everything has become very open, openness being the modern quality, with publicity demanded as a right. It is pleasant to note that men still have some privacy, but this may be part of the swing-over of sexual characteristics. Shopwindows, advertisements, show women so exposed, that a woman can feel all is seen, all is known. Present-day openness can be called healthy and natural, or unseemly. It is a matter of taste, and taste is changing rapidly. But one has to realize that as woman has become more public so has everything else.

All through history woman has represented the hidden side of life, but now nothing must be hidden. These enormous social changes in her position must indicate a change in woman herself, as well as a change in much else. We see her being free, for it is so public a thing that her freedom is very clear to us, but what we do not see is the effect of her freedom on men. This is still a private thing.

It is no longer entirely her position as wife and mother that gives her meaning, for the more she becomes herself the less she lives by these functions. They are now her private life. If it is no longer her deepest relationships for which a woman lives, this is so new a thing that it is almost as though nature itself is changing, and we are all so busy living it that we hardly take it in. But does it not mean that woman, who has always been confined, is now almost without confines, which can on occasion mean that she hardly knows where she is?

She used to be beside man. She lived through man. She took the shape of the life his abilities created, and half created for her sake. All her energies were expended in furthering his well being. The qualities that were called out in her were those that helped him most. She does this less now, and the difference in her, and to her, and to him, is very great. Her living for herself and for her work, as a man does, has quickened in the last hundred years, and it has changed the fluctuating pattern within which woman has been held.

Man has always made the social pattern; he has evolved the dominant idea, and woman has lived within his pattern, and done her best to believe in his ruling idea. Now neither the first nor the last is entirely true. A woman has always had to be guaranteed, for without some family background she was suspect, but now she needs a guarantee much less, for it is frequently her work that explains her.

Of course a great gift has always permitted a woman to live in her own right. But now her achievement, her profession, her means of livelihood place her and explain her. These changes are so general that one watches with deep interest as she maintains her new role, wondering how it will develop, and what it costs her to keep it going. The social gain is clear, and at times it is very impressive, but if there is a loss where is it—is the price high—and who pays it?

Woman's emergence has come at the same time as our marked collectivity, our drift toward crowd values, our belief in an equality so loosely and widely held that it resembles a passionate longing, more than a belief, that everyone and everything shall be as alike as possible. It is an attitude that almost assumes all differences are unfair and only similarity is truly just.

The old belief in a sturdy independence, with hard

work, enterprise and hardihood thought good and necessary if one was to prosper or even to survive, made life a struggle that was unequal and too hard for many. We lived both its badness and its goodness, and we now live the reaction from those cruelties of competition. We seek our good in oneness. We have swung from a belief in enterprise to a belief in compassion, and we are living every side of that. Are we perhaps serving a new value of wholeness? There is as yet no clear answer, but our emotional decision is against barriers of any kind. Individual differences are resented, we must be intimate with all, open to all, and so we tend to grow more and more alike.

The radio and television are used not only to distribute news, information, and entertainment, but also to establish a tribal atmosphere; everyone using Christian names, everyone surprisingly fond of everyone else. It all seems to say, and this must be what we want to hear it say: "We are all one, and nobody has anything to fear." Now this is surely a maternal atmosphere—giving reassurance, keeping everyone close and safe as a loving woman would.

It is also the reigning sign of society at the time of woman's emergence, so that she issues forth into a society that tries to be like a happy family. It might be said that if women now stand on their own feet, exist in their own right, support themselves, live alone in their own flats, they are partly able to do this because they are now contained in our modern collectivity; protected by, even living through it instead of living through men.

The new collectivity of women makes them resemble each other almost more than they did when each lived by adapting herself to the highly individual ideas of one man. They no longer have to believe that the views of one man constitute normality, no matter how surprisingly they differ from the views of other men. It comes near to meaning that woman is no longer caught in man's fate as she has always been. Many women now think as the crowd thinks, and they believe in crowd opinion. It makes them free of individual claims, and they may perform fewer of those incredible feats of adaptation that they once accomplished out of loyalty to the man who needed them, but it makes the women seem a little anonymous.

Society has taken on many things that women used to do, the care of the young and the sick and the old, the necessary care of the individual. So strange are the shifts of modern times that not only are women less feminine, less confined in their homes, but it is now society that has become feminine. Social legislation has taken on much of woman's former role, social feeling includes and comforts all, and crowd manners are warm and welcoming.

Our need of drawing together, our seeking for oneness, takes place in an era of universal dread. Our power to destroy is now limitless. Within the last fifty years we have learned the extent of our power to do evil, and we are rightly frightened. It is even possible that we are now afraid to be ourselves, that we want to become indistinguishable one from another, that we need to be lost in the crowd. The crowd has become the mother with whom we can feel safe.

If femininity has gone out into society, partly out of woman's keeping, some of it has passed to men who now live it in their own right, both nobly and ignobly. Women may be drawing masculinity from men, though sometimes it feels as though masculinity were being passed to us, almost forced on us, and we do not want it. We ask men to help in not letting us take more than our right share. Even though it seems certain that femininity must be newly defined, we do not want to substitute masculinity for it. Yet in these puzzling shifts and changes it is possible that as we take on so much masculinity we weaken men, drawing their masculinity from them by our aggressive strength. We feel grave concern, for there are times when we are so strangely neuter that no one can reach us, and even to ourselves we are almost lost.

2

Feeling Is Our Cinderella

SOCIETY may lack clarity and even honesty in its concept of woman. The very word is equivocal, and leaves us uncertain who is meant; someone very good or very bad, or hardly there at all? Someone as trustworthy as a rock, or as fluid as water? Someone who is entrancing, or usefully matter-of-fact? Each of these qualities is represented by many women, and some women find they must be each quality in succession, and—on occasion—all of them at the same time.

It may be that woman has, of necessity, remained much less differentiated than man, and though men have formed into one new shape after another while evolving the dominant idea of each age, woman has by comparison remained formless. Perhaps she has had to remain formless, and this may to some degree still be true.

The situation resembles a Chinese play, in which wonderfully garbed actors carry on the drama, while property men wander about the stage doing what is needed, offering sustaining cups of tea, but unimpressed and out of the picture. Men are like the actors who carry the full weight of the drama, while women have much of the property men about them. The Chinese accept the two as being properly together, but in real life it is all different. Women are often thought to show too much, and we are now told that we should notice the drama, whereas we used to be told that it was not our business, except of course to keep it going. We are aware that we cause shouts from the audience, which must mean that we do not give satisfaction, and which could mean that we do our work badly.

Woman has for long dealt with the untidy side of life, affording in private the relief of being natural. It is usual for her to concern herself with the things that should not be seen, and that give away our incorrigible humanity. Yet she is also the show piece, the orchid in the buttonhole, the final flourish of decoration. She is—on a higher level—the altar of completeness and the symbol of a fullness seldom reached. So she cannot be glanced at without her being instantly seen as the kaleidoscope she is, or more properly the paradox she is. So no wonder that she is difficult to define. And let it be said at once that it is most uncomfortable to be a paradox, since it requires great perfection of balance to live it well.

Now that woman has emerged into prominence she has brought with her much that has been long ignored. The new is seldom welcome, and if it is not new but only newly noticed, it may well have the compressed and mis-shapen look of something long packed away. So that airing is advisable.

This may be the time when a better balance between the masculine and the feminine is taking place. This is something of even greater significance and of wider meaning than a better balance between men and women, desirable as that would be. This great possibility is only beginning to show itself, and it is still too undefined for anyone to lay down laws as to what will come. We would be insensitive to a great stir of life if we did not offer the welcome of an open mind, but we would be insensitive to both meaning and value if we did not have grave forebodings, since the issues are great.

Few of us can have escaped knowing at second hand if we have been fortunate, and at first hand if we are just ordinary people, some of the misunderstanding that lies between men and women. Many of us have become aware of the conflict between the masculine and the feminine that exists in our own natures. This is a whole world of new awareness affecting both men and women. If one does not meet it in oneself, it is so flagrant in society that we cannot fail to notice the woman driven by her masculinity and the man sunk gracefully or inertly into his feminine side. These things are inescapable, indeed they are even characteristic of our time. The arts can offer shelter to men lamed by the upcoming of their own femininity; unwilling to take this side of themselves seriously, even fearing it greatly, they honor in music or painting the union of feeling and thought. Yet unable to bring about this oneness in themselves, they sometimes appear to serve value as pale priestesses.

We have every reason to be aware of the tension between thought and feeling, of the extreme one-sidedness of the intellect, which can go so far that one longs for adequate feeling to complement thought. On all sides we see extremes of behavior turning into their opposites. We are chilled by the aridity of the highly specialized thinker, cut off from his feeling and seeking it in tawdry companions and sterile ideals. We cannot help but note the man who lives his active, directed life with such disregard of his own feeling, and of the feelings of those around him, that he breaks down into the morass of his neglected feeling, and is sometimes lost in his own undifferentiated softness.

We see women who are very fluid, very feminine, and who pour out their feelings like an engulfing cataract. They ensnare in the excess of their emotion, they are immune to reason, hurt by demarcation, and they ward off hardness and clarity as though these were the evil that their love must deny. But behind the torrent of their softness is an implacable will to power, and what affects those about them is not their softness but their tyranny. No one can escape some encounters with these many extremes of behavior, each displaying clearly its own striking contradiction; nor can we be blind to the revolt among families and friends. We all begin to understand each other so well that we feel a mounting need of understanding ourselves. Why do we behave as we do, and why will others not see themselves as we so cleverly see them? It is an old predicament, but now our eyes are being helped to open.

Explanatory terms are difficult to find, and there may well be objections felt at calling feeling feminine and thought masculine, since it is obvious that men feel as well as think, and that women think, though infrequently, as well as feel. The terms are teasing, but attitudes and attributes have been roughly grouped in this manner for a long time. A man in a fussy, indeterminate mood is called womanish, while a woman's vigor and dominance calls out such sayings as "The gray mare is the better horse" and "It's clear who wears the trousers."

There is a further symptom of our times that is relevant to our subject, and this is the constant talk of relationship. In politics, in psychology, and in industry, relationship is spoken of as a thing in itself, an essential thing which if ignored disturbs organization, and easily ends negotiation. The bond between people has come to be regarded as the precious bridge across which reason and trust can pass. It is as though we have become so conscious of the division between individuals, of their lonely uniqueness and baffling difference, that all hope of communication and security now rests on our ability to relate consciously to one another. We see that thought implies defined difference and so brings cause for conflict, unless feeling creates a bond wherein some sameness may be discovered.

If we remember that women have put all they are into creating relationships, that the joy and suffering of maintaining the close personal tie has been their side of life, almost their greatest gift and creation, then we might go so far as to say that not only are we in the midst of the emergence of women, with its threat and its promise, but that we are living in a nascent feminine age. The present concern with human behavior and with the relations between people is essentially a feminine concern, and it is one more indication of society's present gender.

It is doubtful wisdom to generalize so loosely, but it is sense to say that our present world offers many signs that the feminine is rising to take its place beside the masculine on new terms—that thought has evolved so far that it needs clarified feeling to balance it, if thought is to remain the safe guardian of our human fate. We are forced to believe that thought needs to be partnered by feeling that is as clear as thought, and perhaps the recognition of this is the real emergence of the feminine. It is a birth that may bring much good, but which is difficult to achieve, since no one is wholly convinced of its value.

Feeling is under a great handicap which must be admitted and examined. The handicap is that the quality of feeling cannot be proved, but only recognized by feeling of equal quality. If true feeling is the precious value that must be given place, how are we to learn to assess it truly? The difficulty of recognizing and honoring feeling is part of the disability of being a woman, and part of the intangibility of the feminine principle. So we are faced with a profound need of something we cannot measure, indeed can barely describe, but whose presence or absence changes everything. Let us not try to define it yet, hoping that its quality may declare itself later, only stating that true feeling is rational and life-giving, and that its function is to assess value.

Thought, on the other hand, has every advantage, for thought can be tested with facts, figures, and logic. Thought can quickly be shown as false or true, constructive or subversive. Even when unrecognized emotion distorts thought it soon becomes clear what has happened. The thought grows increasingly prejudiced and it is seen that this is so. Men know where they are with thought. Thinkers may differ in their ideas, do differ profoundly, but they can search out the point of difference and battle for clarity. Reason knows when it rests solidly on proof, and when thinkers venture into speculation, they know that time may force them to retreat. They know how difficult it is to keep reason clear of preference and blindness, but this is their avowed aim, and they have created sufficient order in thought to make it clear why they can respect and trust reason.

But feeling—what a Cinderella this is! It is feeling that most women live by, and it is the quality that women are wanted to represent. Perhaps our greatest failure is when our feeling is untrue, and our constant predicament is the painful obligation of disregarding feeling. If a woman says that an act is against her feeling, or that her feeling tells her that something is right and good for those concerned, she may, by her true interpretation of the feeling-situation, give a man access to his own feeling. Then he can view the situation anew, and live it more fully and truly. When a man is in relation to a woman who possesses this quality he has a heightened sense of life. She has related him to his own feeling, and intangible things have fresh vigor. He knows, though not with his head, that when a woman has done this, every act both great and small has zest and reality, proportion and harmony.

But there is always the danger that a rapport with feeling may not be recognized, it may be flouted, and it can easily be lost. A change in place will bring out different sides of the character of both in a relationship; or their being joined by a discordant third person may bring disunity. An unavowed falsity in either can chill feeling, can even end its power to function. Feeling was there alive and stimulating, and then discord paralyzed it, and after a time it had gone. So how can one trust it, how can one be sure that it truly existed when it seemed to be present? The harmony may seem to be true feeling when it was only caprice or unreal sweetness. A man lends himself to it, and it turns out to be no more than childish love of power, or an evasion of reality blurring sense, ignoring the rigor of outline.

One can then say that the man's feeling was not sufficiently true to assess feeling truly. But men so often do not know what they feel, are afraid to face their feeling, and when woman dares not be true to what she feels, thinking that for safety's sake she must mirror the man's feeling, then feeling as true assessment is unowned and absent. The resulting confusion is constant enough to make both men and women despair; for if we do not feel what happens to us, we have not lived our own experience. We have not been ourselves.

But men are taught to give heed to their heads not to

their hearts, and they have every reason to be wary of feeling-judgments. It is understandable why men often fail to recognize the just claims of feeling, and it is perhaps also understandable why when they know true feeling is present they put impossible burdens upon it, trusting it to suffer all. And need we question that when the woman possesses true feeling and the man knows that she does, he values it beyond all else?

As men trust to objective thought and have made of it a just measure, they are chary of the very word feeling, and their distrust of women is partly rooted in the intangibility of the feeling she represents. Men are rightly afraid of feeling judgments that only entangle them in minutia, lead them into the irrational, or involve them in distasteful unreason. For no one can say where the just sense of feeling ends and the heat of emotion begins.

What we all know in our hearts, and recognize in others instantly, but in ourselves reluctantly, is that emotion is fed from irrational sources. Emotion boils up from unadmitted depths, usually uncontrolled and often uncontrollable. It may render the human being in whom it arises helpless as well as terrible. It can be a cry from the depths of our nature, an outburst of long-banked fires, rightly dreaded in their accumulated heat. Emotion is so incalculable that hate can be close to love, and kisses and blows come in quick succession when emotion is molten.

All this we know to be true, and at some time in our lives most of us have known it in ourselves. Yet it is true that feeling which is not emotion is as reliable as thought, that it assesses value truly, and keeps a living relation to experience. Above all it lets life flow healthily, for it allows movement and the entry of the unexpected. Such feeling might be said to have the quality of creating life, and it could also be said to relate the disparate. It is as though feeling perceives connections truly, is aware of differences yet maintains a bond between opposing things. Perhaps bond is a word denoting too tight a hold to be truly descriptive of feeling at its best; for feeling seems to recognize what is present, and holds it in relation, making a whole of it from very compassion of understanding. It may be that feeling has detachment, aware of that which is not itself, aware of the opposing thing and of the suffering entailed by difference. Feeling can endure the tension of the opposites, can accept their incurable contradiction, and by its acceptance and containment it can relieve some of the tension.

Where feeling is true there is a rational order, and a clear-sighted acceptance of contradiction; also—feeling blends pity with irony. Even though we are unable to catch feeling in any proven law, we all know from experience that when insistence and imposition are lacking, opposites move closer together and some interchange becomes possible. When thought has failed to bring this about feeling may accomplish it.

Though we are dealing with something essentially evasive, even attempting the nonsensical thing of thinking about feeling, and so finding every word inadequate, our hearts can tell us beyond argument that feeling is as real as peace, and as valuable as meaning. That it is usually unstated when present, and that it is always at the mercy of recognition. If no one is aware of its presence it still has value. If it is denied it is still a hidden kernel of sense. The fate of feeling has something of the fate of the feminine, which can be ignored and outraged or protected and honored for like qualities.

Now, how convenient it would be, how restful and satisfactory, if all women possessed this feminine quality of feeling. But sadly enough it is not so, for countless women lack it, and many men possess it to perfection. One is not born a feeling type because one is born a woman, and one is not born a thinking type because one is born a man. Feeling in men is often fresh and life-giving. Men's feeling is seldom overused, while women know that feeling is expected of them, and so they ape feeling which they do not possess. They turn out false feeling automatically as the trade jargon of their sex. Many women are born with inferior feeling, feeling that is blunt and insensitive, and how much help have any of us had in the training of feeling? It has long been the denied value though now it meets with honor.

We have to accept the unpalatable fact that life is not so neat that it grants true feeling to all women, nor clear thought to all men. Let us open our hearts and admit that these are but terms for attributes we seek to understand, and that we may have to suffer to gain. When we call feeling precious we must accept that it is in the keeping of men as well as women. We each need it in ourselves and in the other. If today many men have seen that feeling is essential, and have developed a subtle sense of individual quality, and women have fallen under the spell of thought and seek it as their source of honor, both these things are the new exchange still full of novelty for all.

3

Existing and Not Existing

T H I S book is an attempt to understand what women have been in the past, and who they are becoming now that they have a new ability to change. Women are very varied, though not so varied perhaps, and certainly not so defined as men. One woman differs markedly from another, so that any generalization that is made will be untrue of most, but true of a few. Many generalizations will have to be made, and there will be many a statement of a half truth; but women are difficult to catch in a single concept. Perhaps their chief problem is that though they differ as individuals they are all expected to play the same role of adaptation to men; yet as they differ in themselves they must also differ greatly in their capacity to adapt to others. Because they are women they are usually expected to make a home, which requires practical ability and a discerning heart. Of course many are bad at it and are condemned accordingly. But if every man because he was a man had to build his own home, and continue to build it day after day, we would surely sometimes hear a cry of "But I'm not a natural builder."

What does make women one is their bodies, for their bodies imply that the basic experience of a woman's life will be her relations with men and with children. Yet even this may not be entirely true, for though a woman may not receive and give life physically she may do it wholeheartedly in every way except the biological. So a woman can be completely woman with her heart and mind, but not with her body.

Yet one still has to say that it is her body that makes her woman, and that her bodily relations with men and with children influence her entire life. Whether she has such relations or whether she lacks them affects her own development. Society tends to judge women biologically, and she even judges herself biologically as though her body was the important thing about her. She is spoken of as someone who has had, or not had, a husband or husbands, a child or children, a lover or lovers. These are the facts of her life, and they have made her what she is. She may also of course have made the men and the children what they are, but that is less considered.

Woman is born into her paradox, she is caught at the very beginning by an unanswerable query: "Does she live for these relationships, living as a function in the lives of other people, or does she exist in her own right?" Well— does she exist in her own right, and if so how much? A man lives in his own right and he must, for all our chances of order, stability, and innovation depend upon his independent vigor. But does a woman exist in her own right, and does she want to, and does anyone else want her to? And how much harm does she do to herself when she proves that she can? Here lies her paradox, the knife edge of contradiction on which she balances. It is said that when you reach the acute discomfort of the paradoxical that you are near the truth. Then the truth must be that women represent a contradiction.

Let us accept this for the moment and agree that women both do and do not exist as themselves; with this gadfly of an idea put behind us, we are now in the feminine labyrinth and must proceed with caution. If women live through men, receive their basic experience through men, what is the effect of living through and by and for other people? This in itself may be the central experience of woman. If you live for other people it is not precisely the same as existing solely for them, as though without them you did not exist. But it has at times been thought of in that way, and indeed it can have that result. Partly that is, but not altogether. Many societies, many men, and some women would say that women exist for men, for their support, and their happiness. It is both a satisfying and an appalling idea, and either reaction is understandable.

We then have to inquire whether man needs woman to live entirely for him, requires nothing less from her and cannot do without her. We will postpone the answer until we are sure what it is, and we will not even glance at the possibility that many a man would be amazed at the idea that any woman lives for him, since it seems more true that his every effort goes into appeasing her imperious will. We will ignore the validity of the man's amazement and ask: "Is it possible to live entirely for another person?" We might add: "Would anyone be able to endure our doing it?" But that question is pointless, for we know they can and do endure it; they even like it when it is done well.

There are so many facets to the role of living for others that they must be taken in turn. The effect on women of the long-held view that women should, and in fact do, live for men and for children has been so marked that it practically obscures woman as she is in herself. This commission laid on her could explain all her good qualities and all her bad. All her heights of devotion are the logical result of living for others, and so is her waywardness, her witless vagary, and her wit. For she is saying in countless ways: "If I do not exist this is what it is like," or: "If I belong to you then tell me who you are," or: "Will nothing I do make you see the folly of what you ask?"

If now in our strange modern times—modern times are always strange as proof of their modernity—women are expected to stand on their own feet but to go on living for others as well, it is only natural that they suffer much inner confusion. At times they feel split in two by their submission, as much as by their protest and refusal. That modern women are split in two is the real basis for these reflections.

It is time we reminded ourselves that women are masculine as well as feminine. This of course is true psychologically as well as physically, and modern psychological thought now takes it for granted. Both men and women carry a dual inheritance, and we have to take into account the masculine side of the woman as well as the feminine side of the man.

To look into this duality at all thoroughly will cause us to examine the natures of each, and we must risk getting lost in the mazes of definition, as well as hopelessly puzzled by the mirroring back and forth of reciprocal prejudice. Though women are our subject, it seems necessary to refer frequently to men, as men and women are so often measured by the qualities of the other. As well as being judged by the preferences of the other. When they are in relationship they reflect each other until one can hardly say which qualities belong to each, and when together they may be more themselves than when alone. Together they may create the third quality of heightened being for which they then both live.

Withdrawn from each other they change markedly. One supposes that men when together are more masculine. One knows that they may do their best work, rise to their greatest achievements when away from women. But though at the peak of their masculine fortitude and skill when without women, they may then live some aspects of their own feminine natures. Under severe strain and in special circumstances, where men are deprived of action and forced to live passive endurance, their faces take on a look of feminine patience and devotion, as though the feminine in them had helped them keep vigil. This can be seen in photographs of explorers, or mountaineers, or of many a man who has undergone an ordeal so severe that both sides of the nature were needed to meet the challenge.

The feminine nature of man shows in small and in great ways, from the knitting of sailors, to the androgyne quality of celibates, from the tenderness of the compassionate man, to the creativity of the artist. Men are often forced to some expression of their feminine side when there are no women to relate them to that side of themselves, and the morbid aspect of this subject is much discussed. When the feminine side of the man is infantile, still in need of the mother, still partly held in the primitive oneness of the unconscious, then he is not sufficiently masculine to be able to relate to women. He is compelled to turn to his own sex, seeking to augment that which he lacks in himself. This may afford a release from the claims of maturity which neither partner could face alone, but that it is an evasion of wholeness is certain.

Within recent years we have begun to accept the duality of our natures, but we do not wholly like it, and we have hardly yet realized the creative results of integrating both sides. Psychological knowledge leaves little doubt that man only becomes wholly masculine when he is in possession of his own femininity, and woman is only wholly womanly when she has taken her masculine consciousness as the crown of her development. But this is further than most of us have reached. We are only at the stage of noting that women no longer want men to live their masculinity for them; and we also wonder how much men still need us to live their femininity. It is already clear, however, that we can help each other greatly by becoming responsible for the latent sides of our natures. It is even clearer that we become very strange people indeed when we live our latent sides with blind determination, unconscious of what we are doing.

Women seem to need to live in a personal relation, and they tend to lose their naturalness when without one. Living together in large groups often distorts women. The modern institutional life, such as that of great hospitals, universities, industries, and defense services is still fairly new for women, so that it is too soon for them to have found their own pattern. They tend to copy masculine ways, and they have not yet evolved forms to contain them, as men with a longer experience have done with such brilliance.

The splendid uniforms, the ritual courtesy that men create in religions, courts, ships, and armies could be called an expression of ordered feeling, which then contains and enhances their every act. It is—if one cares to look at it so—the containing feminine. The rich world of intricate rules, garnered meaning that marks value, is a masculine achievement of a high order, and only done on a smaller social scale by a few women.

At present when many women are together masculinity emerges almost as a defense against any show of feeling, as though women are honored to serve an idea, and render themselves austere the better to do it. Authority does not suit women when it imitates a man's call to hardness, and it is our handicap that we often have to be fierce to be firm. That we can be fierce is certain. The energy of a woman can be terrifying, and it hardly needs saying that we can be unbridled tyrants, our frankness breaking all bounds. That great woman St. Teresa of Avila was a cyclone of energy, bending all before her will, kind and incorrigible, and she even reproved God himself, saying: "You have few friends because you treat them so badly."

We indulge with our feminine side, for femininity always hovers near to indulgence, and then we call up our masculine side to hector and punish. As the masculine forms of discipline sit ill on most women, it is possible that we will have to find a way to live in large groups that has more of graciousness and less of discipline. Then collective living may not distort the individual woman out of ordinary recognition. Perhaps we must give over our effort to handle large numbers with military efficiency —though we have never attempted its strangest contortions—and teach manners of the heart; resting feminine order on courtesy to the individual. One might—as speculation—go so far as to say that it is for woman to find a way of saving the individual from sinking into the herd, for when the personal relation is lacking it is herd value and behavior that appears in its place.

When a woman assumes responsibility for large groups it is a severe test of her power to remain a person, for when she works from her masculine side she may become formidable in a way that is out of all proportion to the occasion. Almost as though our masculinity is not personal as it is in a man, but as though we drew on the deep fund of masculine force in our unconscious and live it without discrimination, under the illusion that it belongs to us. If we are to avoid this and maintain a balance that is bearable for us and for others, then there seems little doubt that we must balance both sides of our nature, keeping close to feeling, and serving order with our understanding.

Fortunately when we relate to the impersonal within us we are less under the spell of the impersonal outside us, even remaining happily human in its presence. When this is achieved, and it is achieved and always has been, it can be so good that it is a worthy goal for women to move toward. If it is touched on so early in our argument it is to give us hope, when the matter we consider has less promise.

4

The Masculine and Feminine Principle

THIS talk of masculine sides and feminine sides of the character as though both were clearly defined, and everyone could see and feel them distinctly both in ourselves and in others, may well arouse some protest. The protest would be justified, for the more one ponders this subject the more it is seen as a constant exchange. Men and women pass strength and weakness back and forth to each other. Hardness and softness appear and disappear in both. We live the truth that every quality is sometimes good and sometimes bad, until our wits are addled and we are driven to seek further understanding.

There might be further protest expressing the general distaste aroused by the crude labeling of psychologists, who with far too much assurance trample among the mysteries of human personality. This sense of outrage is understandable, having reason and taste on its side, yet I am convinced by many years of psychological work that experience of the structure of the psyche can bring about a new integration of personality. Analytical psychology has shown that man is masculine outside, with his unconscious personified as feminine, while woman is feminine outside, but with so much of the masculine in her unconscious that it can and does blow her about with the passion of a gale. These findings have now been widely tested and can be taken as a starting point in a search for knowledge of ourselves.

We do not have to go far afield to see that the less a woman recognizes and honors her masculine side the more primitive it is; often explosive and violently unreasonable, sometimes withering her into an arid pedantry, yet often gallantly if excessively heroic. While a man's unadmitted feminine side can keep him evasive of hard reality, making him childish and clamant for ease, seeking everywhere the indulgent mother who will let him remain unborn. Inertia is his greatest problem, and in that stillness he avoids the differentiation he has turned from.

Both men and women are acutely sensitive in these matters, as both imagine they should be completely masculine or feminine, and could be if the other sex would let them; each is outraged to have a doubt cast that this is less than true. But if we do not admit the duality of our natures, then inevitably the unadmitted side is only too apt to be inferior, and we are rightly humiliated when it lives us in spite of ourselves. This is a very prickly subject, involving the frank admission of owning that part of ourselves of which we are least conscious, that part that lies greatly in the unconscious. Only a conviction of the rewards that clarity may bring make one dare to approach it at all.

Since there seems no escape from using the terms masculine side and feminine side as though they were definite things, things on which we all agreed—which is true in a profound and widely inclusive way—these terms must be defined. It may be foolhardy, winning small agreement, but it can hardly be avoided. So—fully conscious that I skirt the morass of ambiguity—I take my first step by saying that masculinity moves toward a goal. I follow other psychologists here. Masculinity gives life. One can say that masculinity acts, so a change takes place, and something new has been defined. Then he who acts has to become responsible for his act, opposition must be faced, because a former pattern has been broken. Standing by his act he has to become an individual, one against many, capable of the thought and force that are required by the new thing he has defined.

The taut bow and pointed arrow of the masculine principle were needed if civilizations were to be born, and life was to move forward. Perhaps man's greatest need was to separate himself from the feminine, the maternal oneness. In order to create himself he had to discriminate the masculine from the feminine, to discriminate against the feminine, knowing its formlessness to be his greatest enemy.

This struggle took many forms in many periods. The beginning, the preconscious, could be called feminine, but slowly men evolved laws making sharp definitions, and laws became sacrosanct. Vices and virtues separated, and the spirit was above us, and our instincts were beneath. The body born to die sought the immortality of the spirit, and the division between the two was a clarity, perhaps the great victory. Slowly the power of the instincts was half surmounted, until painfully though incompletely the division between the soul and the body was accomplished.

This division occurred in the soul of man. He fought for and found the spirit, and in his religions all heavenly things, the sky, the sun, and even God himself were seen as masculine. Man needed it to be so, and perhaps life needed it to be so. It is certain that the division of two such great opposites created a center where thought became possible; a center where one could withdraw from the dangerous encroachment of the instincts. This meant that man had begun to know his own opposites in his own nature, and could grow strong in his own individuality.

But this had a laming effect on woman, and it may be that she still carries the wound. As the patriarchal religions gained ascendancy over the matriarchal religions, she became the lower half of life. She even became the temptress of man; she could not approach the spirit, and man was the intermediary between her and God. Man's need to see woman as a source of evil for man, and so near to evil in herself, could not help but play a decisive part in forming the character of woman, and influencing her attitude toward herself. She still quivers under it, and seems to be still dazed by the contradictions it implies.

It would not be surprising if this were one of the deep

wells which feeds woman's anger, and contrariness and doubt, for these are the qualities of the excluded and dishonored. From this well may also arise the spring of woman's compassion, her patience, selflessness, and insight, the qualities of those who know need, and who answer need; who watch and succor the life and death struggle of men, knowing that all woman has to give is needed.

While women helped they did something more, for they contrived to ignore the paradox they had to live. The paradox that is rooted in sexuality. For she was taught that the sexuality she represented was evil, while the man who loved her said that her sexuality was his greatest good. She was urged by those in authority to be most virtuous, as the body was a vile thing, and woman was the body. She was the body all alone, as it were. This contradiction, this meeting of joy and sin in woman, is part of her essential quality. Women accept it and live it, but somewhere it creates a discord in us, a discord in our blood that makes us ill at ease with ourselves. It puts a drop of poison in us, and will, until we take on this great contradiction both for our own sakes and for that of men.

It is of course the universal wound in the human soul caused by the conflict between the body and the spirit, as real for men as for women, but it has a special bearing on women. If I have come quickly down the ages, merging times and periods, it would have helped but little to pause for accuracy; the way is scattered with records of this discord in life, the discord at the very point where women enter life.

It is a conflict so great that it amounts to nothing less than the struggle between good and evil as it is played out between men and women. It is a struggle where the animal in either can make them both lower than animals, plunging them into self-hatred and self-disgust. But it is also the struggle where tenderness and love create happiness, and an indescribable oneness. These heights and depths are represented by woman, and she typifies the painful doubt as to whether each will be at his best or his worst. It is she who calls out good or bad as though she was the very touchstone of meaning, until this great conflict is almost considered her fault, as though she had created it.

Woman's view of the conflict differs from that of man. What we see from our view almost arrests thought, arresting above all thought about man, for we know that he asks us to surmount the conflict, but also asks us not to step outside it. If man is to be consciousness, then woman must—apparently—be life. So she is wanted to remain at the place of greatest vitality, alive in her body and in her heart. Receiving man and—this is almost his deepest claim —so receiving him that he can think well of himself. For it is not only man's body that woman receives, it is his sense of his essential value that is so often in her care. His idea of himself may make him ask her to deny her own existence, and sometimes he asks her to deny that he is what he is. It is what man asks woman to do to truth itself that paralyzes her power of thought. She is stunned by the difference between personal life and public life, between personal truth and public truth, and how can this contradiction be thought out to clarity? It is hard enough to live it.

But in spite of everything the feminine principle has supported the masculine principle, for the struggle was great even when the protagonists were small. Woman has believed in man even when he did not warrant it, and she has endured the further paradox that man needed woman's aid even when he said he was strength and she was weakness. Because of his need and his dearness she has believed in him, though sometimes it was for life's sake more than for his own.

She learned that she is a danger to him because of the weakness that he finds in himself when with her. He comes to her at his peril for she can soften him, she can expose him to his passions, and his childishness, and to all that is most primitive and most formless in him. She exposes him to the unconscious, so how natural if she has been feared for her power over man; feared and scorned and ruthlessly suppressed, she was then left to carry both his sins and her own. While he, much lightened by what he had left with her, went forward to clarify all those impersonal things in which we have half our being.

Man left woman far behind, and he left her almost incapable of thought. Yet it must never be forgotten that love binds some men and women together, contradicting all other contradictions. While women in general were called inferior, any individual woman might carry the symbol of the man's soul, which he said she was. And this was true, for his unknown feminine side in all its rich life was projected onto her, whether as lust or as love. He saw himself in his image of her, and calling it her, feared or revered it.

When woman was man's ideal he asked her to help him live his ideal, which could mean that he at once left her to perform valiant deeds under her banner. The faulty, indissoluble partnership between man and woman has been lived in many ways, the most constant pattern being that he worked outside the home, while she worked inside; she bore his children for him, formed their characters, respected his work, and sometimes did it for him when he could not. It is almost true to say that while man developed specialized interests woman has carried the wholeness that man could not bear to live. Though it is also true that when he is many-sided, she is sometimes the nothingness he does not know he has.

Woman has always been taught that she must respect man's reason, that it is indeed his great gift of reason that marks him as her superior. But here an odd impasse is reached and a revolt occurs. She knows that the reason of man is one of the glories of clarity. But it is this that inflames her, until any approach to reason can seem a thing outraging to woman.

This is not so surprising as it seems, for man's reasoning can, and often does, go over into its opposite where it concerns women. Religions and philosophies say such strange things about woman, that she sees the weakness in the man who could say such things and doubts the validity of his reason. She is frequently astounded at the human outcome of man's reason and is amazed at the jugglery he permits himself to perform with it. Combined with all this is her daily experience of the unreasonableness of man in his relation to her. It is true that a woman seldom follows abstract reason, and her own role being so poignantly irrational, she becomes wary of all reason as though reason itself were her natural enemy.

This knot is so tightly drawn that one hesitates to touch it further, but it may be safe to suggest that there is some sense in woman's enmity to the ordered processes of thought. For thought sometimes has the inevitable fault of ignoring feeling, and when this happens feeling says truly that thought is incomplete, and almost unreal.

This is all very baffling to man, and can make him feel helpless and hopeless, which has its own sadness and irony. Woman knows that in private she can defeat man's gift of reason with the strength of her unreason, and may she not be forgiven the pleasure this sometimes gives her?

One has to admit that the position into which nature and man has put woman is outside reason. She makes it work, how often and how well, but that is because she can harmonize the irrational, out of high spirits and out of tenderness. She can make the irrational transcend reason, resolving all contradictions, melting all opposites into a contained whole; and too often she has to carry the refuse of reason, shamed and entangled by its results. It has to be admitted that she can also live the tangle without a gleam of awareness of what she is doing. Or she protests, for she knows at first hand the dangerous power of the idea.

Her home can be destroyed by the ardor of an idea. We have long been told that Madame Pélissier, the wife of the French potter, saw the floor boards of her home torn up to fire her husband's kiln. Her children were hungry and she had turned into a fury because of her husband's obsession with the making of a hard glaze. She might be taken as typical of the women who only knew that the life of the family was being ruined by an idea. And men have had strange ideas, ideas against life, horrifying, eccentric, and abortive. So wives often fear ideas in their husbands and they fear thought in themselves, for thought can make devotion impossible. So there has been a tendency in women to avoid mental processes, and nature has seconded them here.

But tendencies follow great principles while individuals are small and uncertain, prone to wide differences, making nonsense of laws. So any individual man may very well live in a constant predicament. For life requires great qualities of him and it is his pride to represent them, even when he prefers not to live them. Yet it must be trying for him when women claim it as their natural right that he should always maintain order, and produce his greatness on demand. Many a woman assumes that as masculinity is in charge of the world it should allow nothing to go amiss, and she blames the man nearest if it does. For though we give our lives into the care of men, we forget the sorry truth that men cannot always be strong in character, or clear in thought. Who could? If a man sometimes plays his role greatly, and is the very apex of life, how fortunate! At other times he can be the first to say: "Have a heart!"

After this flickering glance at masculinity, and what

it seems to stand for, and at how man's needs and accomplishments have affected women, dare I now try to encircle femininity? Not as it is perhaps, because of that we are still uncertain, but as it has been expected to be. This could be taken as the second step in search of our subject; not forgetting that we must look for woman both as a mirage in the eyes of men, and as she feels her reality to be.

I would then say that life, and men, ask mercy of women. They ask for generosity, and for the compassion of acceptance. They ask for joy, kindness and blindness, work and forgetfulness. Too often they ask for variety in indulgence. In short they ask for many aspects of love. They also ask to be allowed to stop being strong, and they enjoy not being clear. They assume at times—their bad times—that all these things are nothing less than their right, easy to give, costing nothing; and too often they are blind to the contradiction at the heart of their demands.

Women must for their own sake, and for life's sake, accept and respect men, and we have to agree forthrightly that as a whole men are more highly differentiated than women. Men have gone far in impersonal achievement and in codified thought, and they have created many specialized worlds. It has to be said that they have done nothing less than create the entire outer scene, which makes what goes on behind the scenes such a surprising contrast.

One of the most poignant paradoxes in the life of a woman is that when a man comes to her, he so often comes to recover his simple humanity, and to rest from being at his best. So a woman frequently has to forego his better side, taking it on trust as a matter of hearsay, and she accepts his lesser side as her usual experience of him. This is hard for her, and here her protests can make him feel a need for her mercy. For while she wishes to admire him she may lack the knowledge, and perhaps the intelligence, to understand the side by which he wins acclaim. She sees his collapse into his home, accepts his need of collapse, indeed receives him with every antenna alert, yet she may forego his superiority with regret. She longs to see his greatness, but has to meet the claim of his smallness.

This contrast between what women hear men can be, and what they sometimes know they are, can be a source of woman's destructive doubt. She is so often split between devotion and rebellion that she sometimes plays the role of the modern Michal who laughed when she saw David dancing before the Ark of the Lord, and whose punishment was being made sterile for mocking when she saw David transcend himself.

Can we take it then that man is sometimes less than wholly masculine, and shall we now ask if woman is always feminine? Does she always show mercy and compassion? But these are love, and at its highest level. If these are expected of woman she is greatly honored, for mercy is a divine attribute. Our Lady is merciful, Kwan Yin is merciful. Few religions are without their Goddess of mercy; so somewhere men and women revere each other, hope for, ask, and blindly expect greatness in each other. Seeing what we exchange in our daily life, let us be glad and even awestruck if we sometimes seek a divine completeness in each other.

Once more we would do well to leave great principles, and this time we must take a look at any individual woman. If she is willing to watch herself live an ordinary day, she must admit how seldom she is merciful; how infrequently she gives any hint of knowing love, and how often it is her own masculinity that drives her roughly until she is nearer a dark avenging fury, than she is to an angel of mercy.

We are now almost impelled to believe that there is no knowing when either men or women may be found living from the side of their natures they forget they possess. We may find out more about these latent sides, and why people choose to live them; that both sides exist in each of us is now regarded as a commonplace of human character and we see it lived wherever we look. It used to be said that when the biological side of life had been fulfilled women took on greater firmness of character, and that men softened markedly, so that each by the process of living rounded out their dual natures. But education for women, and the hard conditions of our times, even some new impulse toward wholeness not yet understood, have given the two sides of man and woman a new prominence.

When men or women are hard pressed, tried beyond their strength, then we may see women summon dogged energy, hardening themselves to deny their hurts, and we may see men caught by their own weakness, trapped by too great difficulty, and sinking into what can seem a long sulk. So our duality becomes more obvious and we are seen to live every aspect of our opposing qualities. But when a quality is an asset and when it is a liability— this needs insight and hardihood to discover.

A man's hurt heart and spiritual wound, as well as his childish evasion and moral cowardice, may make him recoil into his feminine side as his final shelter from the danger of living. Or he may do it from greater and different motives. He may, almost unwittingly, seek to explore and expand his own nature, so that he sinks almost gladly into his latent side, needing to claim it, half realizing that he is a cripple until he finds his creative feeling in his own depths.

Many men today show unmistakably that their feeling is withdrawn from the arid aspects of our modern world; and this is true of the best as well as the worst. The split between thought and feeling is a symptom of our times. For feeling has gone down into the undefinable places where the fresh life lies that is so desperately needed. Many men are suffering the ordeal of loss of feeling. They become stark in their abstract thought, hardly able to endure their own bleak detachment or their rudimentary materialism. While those of a softer nature may live their femininity in its poorest aspects, caught in a travesty of all that femininity stands for. But the perceptive man deprived of his feeling, may after much unhappy frustration come to honor it, learning to know it as the true assessment of living value, and essential half of his own wholeness.

While some men are caught in the latent side of their

own natures, many women show a barely smothered anger that is perhaps a just protest at our modern plight. For countless women are carrying heavy burdens hitherto unattempted. They are giving great service to society, but they do it by drawing on qualities which they have only recently made their own, and which one might say they have made incompletely their own. So that in many circles of society both men and women play an uncertain role.

5

The Man in Our Nature

T H E forgotten past forms a basis for many of our assumptions, and this makes it sensible to look back along the road that women have come. All through time they have been contained and protected, after a fashion. They have lived within the family and the group, acquiring the virtues and the vices of those who submit, succor, watch, and learn by what they receive and by what they are refused. Remaining as unformed as those have to be who are not responsible for their lives; needing the fluid morality of those who are not free; but building up the intense reservations of those who must give on demand, and gaining the deep insight of those who see the armor off, yet of whom blindness is still asked.

Woman's role was so often that of bringing a man back to his human roots when he had overreached himself; she was so often the part of himself he denied, regretted, half despised, as well as his vision of what he wished to be.

[52]

Sometimes she was his very touchstone measuring how far he had risen or how low he had fallen. Together with men, women evolved intimate happiness, where there are no questions. Out of her devotion, and her grace, she created an inner safety where the personal blossomed.

These things came to women within social patterns that she had done little to create. If the design broke she suffered, and had desperate need of inclusion. Without protection she was sexual quarry or untrained labor. So that very gradually—it took her all the time we have had —she demanded, within the memory of many of us, to be considered someone in her own right. That was a very brave and a very bold claim. But greater things than feminine wishes had helped to bring it about, for economic history had reached a point where it was generally convenient to have women earning their own living; so—after a little fuss—she was at last allowed to step out into the exposed and often unrelated position she occupies today.

Well—with such a past, such a role, and such a surprising present, what could anyone expect women to do? What does anyone do when in difficulty, when impelled to a great change for which only a small part of their nature is adapted? They call up all their resources, they call up every last man they can, they call up every latent strength they possess. That is precisely what woman has done. She has always needed the strength of man and now she calls on the man within her own nature, and he comes. She has hardly had time to make a pact with him, she seldom gives thought to arranging a marriage granting equal honor to both. For her call to him has been dictated by need and by panic. She shouts down her Castle walls that the Castle is undefended, and up comes every warrior and handyman about the place. Disreputable and most respectable, all answer her call, and then masculinity takes over. It could not have been otherwise.

From then on the woman in the woman hides in some dusty corner. She hates the noise and the combat, and feels wronged if anyone thinks she is making it, but she is. Those she called up from within her are making it, and any man would say that she can on occasion emasculate those whom nature has made men. When one cannot reason with a woman possessed by her masculine side, and very often one cannot, and happily one cannot beat her, then the man nearest to her may know the same helplessness that women have known through the ages. For when a woman will not see that she is possessed by blind forces within her, she is not an individual, she is ruthless nature, and those about her can but wait for the tempest to subside.

But what are we women to do with this inner man? He belongs to us, he has always been a part of us. We have used him at different times in different ways, though perhaps he has never been so out and about as he is today. Now he is almost universally present, sometimes as an honorable, sometimes as a discordant part of our modern way of life. Can we do less than regard him as woman's most urgent problem, affecting her to a degree that we only begin to calculate, and so affecting all about her?

Women could hardly have survived without him

through the vicissitudes of the ages, when he has been the fury within us, as well as our silent and unsuspected partner. Now he is wanted and used, trained and rightly respected; but even when untrained, when crude but strong and heroically willing, he may be the one part of us our families demand in a crisis. Even husbands count on him when he is useful, though of course deploring him when he is not.

It is nonsense to pretend that he does not exist and that we know nothing about him. We are forced to admit his presence, and we must confess that though he can be a very devil at times, we do find him invaluable. He helps us to live our seemly professional lives, but he also disgraces us. He goes on the loose, taking us with him of course, and rages about in a storm of unreason. His noise may be our unconsidered thought, or our rebellion against thought, but his roar is what satisfies us.

It is he who turns the best of wives into Sergeant-Majors. Any honest husband, if he dares, would admit that this can happen; that he is in very truth married to both an adoring wife and a drillmaster, that he is quite incapable of disentangling the two, and has even had to put up with finding the Sergeant-Major in his bed, and was forced to leave him where he lay. We must confess that we call up our masculine side when we want our own way, when we feel we might enjoy a jaunt with our independent will, as well as when our families need to survive by his efforts. For there is no doubt that this firebrand in our natures helps us both in our good and in our bad, and though this has always been true, we are now losing our heads over the man. If our hearts were wiser and kinder we would not let him have his wild way, though the truth is that it is his wildness, that is our joy, our sweet revenge even, and our abandoned retaliation for aeons of false agreement.

It is his strength and his passion that delight us; his roughness and his ruthlessness intoxicate us. Many modern women are drunk with him. He is our depths, and he is the accumulation of all we have been taught we must not be. He is inconsiderate, unlikeable, unkempt, discordant, opinionated, ill-mannered, noisy, dictatorial, harsh, tasteless, and we revel in him. There has been so much life dammed up in women that it feeds the masculine side of her, feeds and fires him, until he is very nearly out of control at times.

But let society take comfort, for the results of having been women are not all bad; some are good, even very good. If in woman's nature there has been a slow passionate garnering of a love of freedom, of independence, of rough speech, and of impersonal activity, there is also keen insight distilled by years of abnegation, and there is a deep fount of generosity. These may save us.

For though our masculine side is blind strength, he is at times our sacred anger, the volcano from which arises our inchoate comment on life, and which one day we may clarify. Which we may have begun to clarify, and which a few among us today, and through all the yesterdays, have known how to voice without danger of burning those about us. In our cooler moods, and fortunately the masculine half of us does allow us cooler moods, it is he who helps us to gain detachment, thus proving himself the broad high road to understanding. Then we have the intoxicating pleasure of training him to think for us, for he can think, clearly and honestly, though we like him so much that we often accept brass from him in lieu of gold.

It is in our use of him that our greatest hope and our greatest peril lies. Our danger which we may not see or solve, yet which becomes clearer every day, is that our hope of a new birth, even our fitness to achieve the cultural task that seems to lie before us, depends entirely on our ability to assimilate and honor the masculinity within us. This is our modern problem, and our solving of it will decide many things.

It is the powerful fellow in our own psychology who robs us of our femininity and who makes us untrue to ourselves. For we cannot evade the problem of being ourselves, nor do we really get rid of ourselves by living for others. We would like to think we become ourselves when we live our masculinity, but we are mistaken, for he is not us, but only a part of us. When he seduces us into becoming him, as he does, and when we fall, as we do and enjoy doing, then we have distorted ourselves, and distorted life; and is it going too far to say that we have become destructive? What we may do to men, and to the pattern of living, by succumbing to our inner man is a thing yet to be measured, scarcely yet envisaged, and hardly taken into account.

That we are so often captured by our masculine self, carried off without any attempt on our part to make terms of surrender, must not be wondered at for a moment. The fellow is very able. He helps us to feel at home with things of the mind, he intoxicates us with ideas until we are exalted with ideas, being little accustomed to so heady a fare. He is sometimes the inflation of the educated woman, until she becomes learning itself, and floats over the heads of all. And what a rest for a woman, what a blissful change! If we are bold he lets us become all knowledge, as though we had invented it recently. If we are timid he makes us become pedantic heads without bodies. If our natures are reckless, this splendid revolutionary lets us be as rough and ruthless as an invading army, and all that we have railed at in men we live in our own persons.

How fortunate, and how much to our honor, that so many women have learned to partner our new love. The women who have faced him courageously and perceptively, who have dared the riches and the humiliations of a real union, have found the rewards to be great. For he can be an administrator and a scholar. He is of course a lively critic, for think of the ages of suppressed criticism he has to draw on. He is a gifted historian, writing with humanity and a warm inclusiveness. Some of the women he inspires have made with him such a mellow whole, that it must be called the very consummation of duality.

But the truth is, and this is our shame, that he will not keep his place. It is in his very nature to protest, dominate, and override. That is why we like him. For he is the masculinity that we have suppressed since time began. He is independence and valor, as well as a crude will to power. He is all this as well as a great impersonal force, stronger, better, worse, and other than we. Those that have experienced his full meaning know that he leads to the spirit.

Yet in our new position, in our new difficulties, he is too often our modern guise. He is us. He lives in place of us, and we are lost. All that used to be recognizably us has now become the slave and chattel of the forceful man in our own nature, who is taking us, not at all unwillingly, in charge. We have long been subservient to men, and now we are craven with the inner man. He bedevils us as much as he frees us. He even causes us to commit a great sin against our own natures, for in his hands we forget the personal, that core from which we all live. Women have always been the guardians of the private and the personal, and if we neglect the quality of these then all our gains may be cancelled by a loss.

6

But Dare We Become Conscious?

A s women become more highly educated, more specialized in their interests, and as more and more of them
enter the professions that require years of intellectual
training, they naturally become increasingly influenced by
their masculine attributes. Women have to summon up
this endowment in order to understand their studies, to
endure the long discipline, and to acquire the weight and
authority their calling warrants.

Such women almost inevitably become identified with
the masculine side of life, and they are very apt to become
somewhat masculine themselves. By looking about us we
see that this is our modern predicament. One hardly needs
to say that it is not an intentional occurrence, and would
be hotly denied by the majority of those to whom it has
happened. But the woman's whole allegiance is given to
a calling evolved by men, requiring a masculine capacity
for thought and purpose; she tends to become her profes-

sional side, for it is precisely here that her pride lies. It is true that men as well as women tend to be formed by their activities. But with women it is still more noticeable, and it often looks as though it is precisely her feminine ardor that drives her to her extremes of masculinity.

It must give her much satisfaction to become so nearly man, for she gains many privileges and much power. Perhaps she also escapes some feminine things for which she had small aptitude, or which she may have scorned. Women have known so much humiliation that it is natural for them to live some of their self-scorn as well as some of their envy. Yet it is in this way that we bring about a grave distortion of our natures, making it difficult for us to live a woman's life; though our professional lives can be admirable, wholly useful and satisfying, so that we gain much that we want, and society gains much that it needs. But a woman can hardly be said to have gained her full independence in this way, for she is usually completely in the power of her masculine side who drives her pitilessly. So she is not free, but helpless in a new way.

As the masculine side of the woman rises from the unconscious it is near to powerful forces that often make a woman behave as though she were more than life size. Powerful and wise women have presumably always existed, and a few of these one supposes could be safely contained in a social pattern. It is doubtful, however, if ever before have such large numbers of women lived the masculine side to such an extreme degree, and so often at the sacrifice of their personal life. Woman's masculinity is like a fire, and certain kinds of fuel make it wax in heat and brilliance. The fuel is varied, old grievances can fire us, and many women are inflammable with gifts and powers left unfulfilled. As men and women are born to a large extent bisexual, having many of the qualities of both sexes, but are then trained to suppress their latent sexual characteristics, these repressed tendencies pile up in the unconscious and this seems to be a time when they insist on being assimilated.

That education so often brings out the masculine side of women must be a signpost that women should regard, but to where does it point? Surely not back to where we were. Education, and above all a university training, is the necessary means of fitting women for professions of impersonal interest, and impersonal honor, and both of these have become very precious to women. An exaggerated value may have been put on them as they are the things that women have lacked, so attaining them makes women feel they are now the equals of men, having reason for equal pride. Many women want to rid themselves of the too personal with its ever entangling emotional claim; and many have been endowed with fine minds and a genuine love of learning, so that they would feel it intolerable not to have the best education they were capable of taking. There seems to be both a wish to live without men in modern women, as well as the will to develop their own gifts. They have found a new loyalty to themselves, and they are willing to pay its high cost. It is a very high cost.

But if education distorts us, is woman's attitude toward education perhaps wrong? Does she falsify herself by giv-

ing learning a false respect, not wanting it wholly for itself but because it has been a masculine prerogative? Is it
woman's attitude toward herself and toward life that
needs a new balance? Or must education itself be hu-
manized for women? This could mean that the emergence
of women would bring about a change in education.

It is not a small thing to have brains and to be told that
it is bad for you to use them. And this happens constantly
to women. It is one of the things that infuriates her.
Women have at present a hunger for the impersonal,
which may not always be genuine, though for many it is
profoundly real. When women give themselves to an impersonal interest they are often told that they have un-
fitted themselves for personal living; that they have become impersonal in the places where it is barrenness, and
informed dullness. That they have not made themselves
more admirable, but less, for they have falsified themselves. And these dismaying words can be true. So women
are confronted with the possibility that an attempt at
greater consciousness, that thing universally praised, may
be harmful for them. Many women have had to face this,
and it can seem the final injustice of their puzzling role,
the outrage that lands them in confusion and suffering,
convinced that it is intolerable frustration to be a woman.

They thought they were doing the one right thing, for
they saw how unconscious women often are. It has to be
admitted that they saw truly, for in woman the opposites
lie close together, and they may lie asleep. Since it has
been woman's fate to remain unconscious much longer
than men, her emotions tend to live her, and her thoughts

take possession of her: for she does not exist enough in herself to have an attitude toward either. But these generalizations can be lying things, and one has to keep them clear of individual men and women; yet it must be said that women as a whole are in a state of natural oneness, that this is where they are expected and wanted to be, though also scorned for being, and when they try to change it, their first peril is that they may cease to be women.

It can seem that unconsciousness is almost represented by woman, as though her role is to live it and to symbolize it for others. It has either been natural to her, or else she has never been allowed to stray far from it, until it seems as though if man is to differentiate his capacities he requires the contrast of the undifferentiated in woman. If she were as differentiated as he, the polarity between them might cease. Or perhaps her being near the unconscious is what makes her transformative to man, and if she leaves her natural oneness she may miss her richest experiences, and so deny man's depths to him.

She finds it strange that she is expected to be unconscious, that it is asked of her and needed from her, that her unconsciousness has even been insisted on by society, and that this was so even when she was blamed for her instinctive nature, her vagary, and her lack of specialized interests. In fact we are blamed for being what we are told we must remain. It may be this that sets us all awry. If society has been right in its feeling that consciousness on the part of woman would upset a balance on which much good depended, then woman must be the spring in which life rises spontaneously, good and bad indistinguishably together; and society feels it would lose a true source of nourishment without this. Then modern woman is doing her best to prove society wrong, and the issue between them is still open.

She sees that when she is near the unconscious she connects man with his creative side, that then she is life-giving, and could she play a greater role than this? The answer should be "No," and yet she hesitates to give it. There are many aspects to consider, so she has many reasons for searching sincerity and searching doubt. She knows that her intellect is rarely as good as that of a gifted man. Yet it can be good and an unfed mind has its own dangers. She knows that her intellect seldom makes a bridge between a man and a woman. When a woman tries to meet a man there, she is very apt to find that neither can cross the icy stream that divides them. Many a woman has found that her thought and her ability have to become her secret sin, which must be concealed, only allowing them to appear in public if artfully disguised. An intelligent woman can be driven to the ruse of offering an idea disarmingly, as though it was something she had picked up by the wayside, and was quite unworthy of owning.

Does it all mean that she must read the signpost as saying that she rightly represents unconsciousness? Is she nature? Can man go far afield if she promises to remain rooted in nature? Is that what she has to do, and for always? Then man's power seems a very delicate growth. But let us not look at that, and only attend to the question we have put ourselves.

Waiting for an answer to this question could land a woman in a panic of protest, and yearning, and fear. The answer has to be created and it may take some time. But the question has caught us, fastened itself in the mind, forcing us to ask further questions of ourselves. Though we are often fearful that we may have done harm, we realize that we are longing to do more, if our change is indeed harmful. The question has stuck in the heart as well as in the mind, for it is nothing less than the whole question of what we are to become, and what road it is safe and good and life-giving for us to follow.

But is this very state of conflict not making us conscious? For this is true consciousness, this painful travail that modern woman is undergoing, and it can do nothing less than create in her a genuine gain in consciousness. Is her feeling doing all this, or is it the masculine thought she has found by copying man that tells her home truths, and that drives her on to discover more? It is impossible to allocate the attack of each, but it is these between them who are awakening her from her instinctive duality to a conscious duality. For this is what has happened to woman. She has become two, feminine and masculine, capable of feeling and thinking, and even of doing both in opposition, and noting the opposition. For now there is someone in between, someone who is herself. It can be no other. She is becoming someone who knows the conflict of her own opposites, and knows that they must both be accepted, and held together; knows that the conflict must be endured, for it belongs to her since it is herself. She knows that there is no other way to be oneself but to stand steadfast, accepting the contradictions in oneself.

If this situation is as general as there are signs of it being, though lying below the surface in most, and only clearly in view in some, then we are justified in surmising that the widespread emergence of the masculine in women is a step, a necessary and threatening step, toward the development of the ego in women; the ego being taken as that point of impact with reality where responsibility for one's own quality begins. Nothing less would make women individuals, and individual is what they have rarely been.

Sexual surrender and identification with the loved object has been woman's role, so to be detached, alone, conscious of her own uniqueness can be very frightening, and it can seem wrong. But then it is the Promethean sin, the stealing of fire from the gods, known more frequently to men than to women: we are told that the way for either men or women to become themselves is to see that their own worst problem is their uniqueness; and that to redeem it is the pattern inherent in one's individual life.

As women have taken a great step forward by living the latent masculine side, this may have been the only way they could discover for themselves that they possessed it, and only by living it badly have they found themselves in their sins. It could mean that women are not far from accepting the heavy and exhilarating burden of their own duality. Women may even be very near to the discovery of that central self that could live both the feminine and masculine side, not honoring one less than the other.

7

We Agree with Our Critics

A NEW inner balance in women might make education and careers safe, and if all this is on the verge of happening, wanting only a few generations to develop, then the spirit of the age must require it. But does anyone else really want it? Not with enthusiasm, and sometimes not at all, for hardly anyone really likes impersonal interests in women. It is still an acquired taste, but once acquired—strong. Some men say that they want their wives to have an interest that is outside the marriage. This may indicate great civilization in the men, and it might lead to a new and formidable challenge to women. No longer wanted to be adaptable, they must now be interesting. Well—it could be tried.

It has to be admitted that intellectual enthusiasm in women can sometimes be a little unreal, more the result of insistency than of genuine interest; which may partly explain why "A Career" can be a mocking term, as though the feeling of society is still against it. So women have to be very sure that they believe in what they are doing, and make quite certain how real their belief is. We often force ourselves to extremes of thought that seem more a proof of courage than of cerebration. Perhaps we are testing our daring in thought, and we often break down a barrier of taste or sense just because it is a barrier. We sometimes have to break down a prohibition that exists in ourselves alone, and our aggression is the greater the more we need release from our own self-doubt.

These things can make us very objectionable, with our weighty voices and our heavy certitude, but we are redeeming our past. At present we have an inordinate respect for the articulate, indeed we are taking up definition just as men feel the need of the unstateable symbol that says more than the word. Our present sins are many, so many that we repeat them again and again like a painful lesson we must learn by heart.

Let us say until it bites home: "We are sometimes compulsive tasters of knowledge, and intellectuality puts a spell on us, just because it is intellectuality. We know it can make us barren, and we often feel barren even while we crave it. But we plead in our defense that it is logical, in the slow logic of the generations, to crave the stimulus of the man's world, for our world has been very dull; no one knows quite as well as woman what it means to live under the minus sign. So our flight from the personal throws a light on what we have had, and if the light is not flattering, it may still be true." Then as we face our mounting self-knowledge we say: "A desire for achievement burns in us. Our greatest danger, making us ask for help, is that we are tempted to supplant love with achievement. This danger is great, for we are caught by the modern living for work, and somehow missing living. We are ready to take half blame, for we see proofs on every hand of a lack of belief in the goodness of life, and often a lack of love."

Women may have to rediscover what they mean by love. Both men and women may wish to make new conditions, and new contributions, for women would hardly be as they are today if they had been able to give and to take love happily. If it had been lived so that one could take it happily. It is a searing criticism of love, of men, of society, and of women themselves that they turn from being women. One hardly knows what to call the illusion believed in by many women, that nature meant men and women to be alike, but somehow bungled women. One must suppose them to be mistaken, and that men and women were meant to be different. Nature could hardly have been so stupid as to make two beings just alike except for their bodily functions, and to make one well and the other badly. If they were utterly different they could not relate at all, if they were not somewhat different they could not combine into a whole. The difference between them must be a potential good, allowing a flow of energy from the positive to the negative, and so assuring the heightened life we all desire. But, possibly because of our modern feeling for equality, some women think it would be fairer if we were all positive, no one negative at all. Lost in such a tangle it is to be hoped we find ourselves in time, discover ourselves as essential value at the center of life, fit to take our place in greatness and smallness—but perhaps this is an excess of optimism.

Woman's effort at present is too big. Doing her work and carrying her home, she also needs to still her own doubts about the feasibility of it all. It is more than the impersonal work we do that makes many of us bleak and hard, for this is what we often are. A woman whose whole life is work is under a constant strain to steel herself to her own unnatural one-sidedness. Few men forego their entire personal life in order to do their work; they are usually surrounded by a family occupied in keeping them human, more—diverting and praising them, and so restoring them to themselves. But too many women, functioning on their masculine side, not only have their neglected womanhood to trouble them, but they lead most unnatural lives. They live alone in homes left empty during the day, with the small comfort given by charwomen seldom seen, or they live among a lot of other women, surfeited with unlived femininity. They often live without men, or love or children. They have to earn their living, that is demanded by necessity and is not open to discussion. An impersonal interest dominates their lives, and they partly want it so, but they may pay the intolerable price of giving up their entire feminine side. So no wonder they may be strange, they often feel strange to themselves. This is not denied, but faced and suffered.

While women thus foster the ego, live from the ego, savoring the delights and deprivations of existing for yourself, they have reasons for being harsh. And let no one say that a fine man sacrifices his ego, since it must be obvious to all that you have to have a thing before you can give it up. Women sacrificed their right to be themselves so long ago that they have forgotten how it happened. They are now striving for that right and they are not yet ready to pass beyond it. Women are creating an ego because it has become necessary to them; their craving for differentiation is both creative and destructive, and it will take a long time to satisfy, for the masculine side of women has the passion of unlived life, and it has the numinous quality of the unknown. It fascinates, and countless women feel that fascination as so strong that blindly, as well as consciously, they seek their own integration.

The change that is taking place in women naturally disturbs everyone. At present men are almost as much at sea about it as women are. Men can feel they have a natural right to something that is being taken from them. Women are to some degree stepping outside marriage, since a side of woman is developing that is itself outside marriage. But as both men and women may have large areas, and often their most creative side, that do lie outside marriage, a new concept of marriage is among us and its presence is making us all uncomfortable. We must apparently enlarge our concept of marriage, as well as deepen it, or else commit what truly seems a sin, though an old sin long established, of keeping the person we love most, less than it was in him to be.

One criticism that could justly be made against us, and constantly is made, is that it is the way we live our masculine side that is objectionable. No one minds our having this side, society having now reached the advanced stage of saying this and trying to mean it, but people cannot abide our being insensitive to what we are doing. Above all they deplore our lack of intelligence about being intelligent. It is all true, perfectly true, and we have to agree with our critics. We do lack moderation, and we do show the witless ardor, the same blind devotion to our impersonal interests that we used to show in our personal relations. We formerly became our husbands, and now we often become our leading interest.

It is our shame, but it could be explained enough to win some tolerance and understanding, for what is happening is that modern woman abandons herself to her masculine side as she formerly abandoned herself to her husband; and with the same blind conviction that she is doing the one right thing. She neither realizes it, nor intends it—it happens to her. She still identifies herself with a cause, or an idea, as she has always identified herself with a person. It has been called love, it is close to devotion, but there is no denying that it lacks all proportion. We are a long way from combining loyalty and detachment. It is fair to remember that attachment has been the only role allowed us, and we have needed a little time to discover that blindness is its other side.

There are things to be said in favor of masculine women, a few things, and one of them is that they have given their masculine side work to do and he does it well. They have demanded his best, and they have made him do work of a high order; while the women who disregard their masculine side, live domestic lives, are surrounded by children, keep all in order except that crude chap who is part of themselves. The rough, noisy fellow in a good woman's nature helps her get through her heavy work, and makes her as staunch as a battalion in support, but nothing will make her see that this rowdy creature exists and is the disorder in her home. Her devotion lets her think only of others, never of herself, it is her very goodness that makes her blind, but she too has a masculine side and he is cruder than the trained partner of the professional woman.

Women spend themselves for others with such generosity that they seem at times rightly outside criticism. But no one is that, and today many women are the mere torn tatters that remain of the fight between their loving self-forgetfulness and their search for themselves. For woman has been caught by a great force. She is in the hands of that side of her nature that can become her understanding, her courage and her wisdom, the spirit in her own soul, but which can also make a horror of her. How much we must have longed through the ages to be men, as we now travesty men and travesty thought when we let ideas drive us fanatically. We have not much experience in giving a considered "No," but we must learn to face our masculine side with a firm refusal, denying his right to live us. It is he who distorts us, and it is he to whom we must learn to relate, much as though we were married to him, as at times we seem to be. He must not be allowed to harry us, or in any way possess us. We have to find the courage to say to him: "You and I are two, not one, but I ask to know you for I need you." It is simple to say, but the accomplishment, even to a small degree, can be sheer torture. To know oneself is of course the work of a lifetime, a lifetime of searing honesty with oneself. And now women, whose essence has been to forget themselves, are asked to notice the extent to which they are men. A woman generally flames with anger, denying the possibility; then she may demand why she should not be a man, and already the boundaries of her consciousness are extended.

She may chance to look in a mirror when possessed by her masculine side, and seeing the fierce light in her eyes can be appalled at its alien fire. Or when she is voicing unreal precepts her child says: "Buzz buzz," and she wonders who was speaking with her voice. Or when she is in a contrary mood, leaving a standpoint the instant she has taken it, her pleasure in bedeviling for the joy of bedeviling, at creating chaos to render the strong helpless, may make her recognize her devil of irrational thought. There are a million ways, all uncomfortable, in which we are introduced to the man in our own natures. A woman can dream of clanking about in a suit of armor, no longer vulnerable but safe and protected, or she can wake in terror because she has dreamt she was dying within a carapace shaped like a Harley Street specialist. Once known, this masculinity has still to be assimilated, and though it is difficult, what else is to save us from our present plight?

A relation to this inner man would seem to be the solution to our problem, and that accomplished a woman may be free to relate to man less painfully. She may see that she turns to her masculinity for her independence of thought and will, but she may not see that because he is partly masculine will to power, he makes her violate her own feelings. If she will not test her thought, or question the aim of her will, she may have gone down a sorry road; for our masculine side is driven by unsuspected forces and we are only beginning to recognize some of them.

He is the great figure we have to face, and without a skin to skin experience of him we are his unconscious plaything. But now we have stern reasons for facing him. Perhaps never before have we been so fitted to see ourselves. We must not think this masculine side an enemy and stop there, believing we have found out all there is to know about him, for then we would have lost the possibility of his great good.

We must go further and see him as our precious partner, our chance of balance, of a new oneness within ourselves, a fecundation from the depths of our own souls. When our heart criticizes our thought, and our thought judges our heart, only then do we begin to have a center where we are truly ourselves, and where our "Yes" and our "No" at last make sense.

Woman's urge to become man is wholly understandable, for it is the masculine that has been regarded as the enlightening, the life-giving power where first honor lay. This truth has been evolved by men, and it is a great truth that must never be forgotten. It is still true when individual man is weak. There is a strong taboo in men,

and in women, against mentioning the individual un-
worthiness of men as though it was a danger. It feels dangerous when it is present.

Women can become so weary of building up man's sense
of his own value that they often try to destroy it, forgetting how necessary it is. Perhaps they sin in this way because their own value is so often destroyed; but even when
most sick at heart they still know that the greatness of the
spirit, the greatness of clarity and order, must not be less-
ened by man or woman.

After aeons of watching men and seeing them at their
weakest, women agree that his very greatest is needed.
Now when we ape men, we still pay allegiance to the
masculine principle, as though only there can honor lie.
Perhaps what both men and women need is to see and
admit their own weakness and grant strength to the other.
That might leave each free to revere great principles. To
make the feminine principle honored, and so lived will-
ingly, may be the future work of women, but they will
need help from men.

8

Our Inferiority

THE effect on women of being thought inferior has been great, and we will not understand women any better unless the whole subject of their inferiority is aired. Women, as a whole, have always been told that they were inferior, there even seems some pleasure taken in telling them so, and this has had varied effects. It has made women charitable and cynical, abject and hostile, and just inferior. Our situation in life is admittedly inferior. We are dependent on man for our most feminine experiences, and we are often dependent on his strength. So our position is one of weakness. It is hardly necessary to say that we have not liked being told that we are inferior, and we are very alert to the restrictions that surround us because of our poor quality.

In the Middle Ages the question as to whether women possessed souls was much discussed by scholars, and outrageous to any woman as the query seems, she sees that it stated the attitude from which women were regarded. They were hardly moral beings. Women were so often deprived of freedom of judgment that there was little morality in any decision they made. They could be obedient or saintly, or summon guile to avoid being a victim, and there was some gain in being a wanton, but many were almost outside the moral problem, and hardly to be taken seriously.

This is part of woman's past, making her wounded and angry, or spoiled and frivolous. With the hurt of ignominy as part of her inheritance, there is at times an Ishmael in her who glares from the surrounding desert—"I stay apart and I won't come in on the terms offered. I won't in fact be a woman if I can avoid it, for in my blood is the agelong knowledge that it isn't safe."

This is a strange thing to find in modern woman, but it is sometimes there. It is doubly strange as the most striking thing about women is that they lose life and meaning if they step outside the personal pact. So they lose when they protest, and like no one else they often lose because they protest. They cannot fight, and they can barely compete. They may win in competition, but they then lose their naturalness, and become odd as women. So the painful fact is that one of woman's greatest difficulties is that in taking action she may alienate man. This is so apt to happen that she bludgeons and placates. When she remains passive she can hope to remain within the personal pact, but if she acts on her own she easily steps outside it. Then enmity between man and woman can come so easily. As though independence in a woman angers man, upsets the polarity between them, does on occasion such damage that our masculinity can seem the violation from which at all cost we must be saved.

When men and women are at variance any level of discord may be reached. She may storm hoping he will force her to behave, or the lowest level of all may give horrid sense to the music hall joke of "He no longer loves me enough to beat me." For when a woman is possessed by her masculine fury, and she is beaten, the man has rescued her from a dreadful form of her inner power. Her relief is seen as contemptible, but she could feel grateful that someone is stronger than her own power devil, and has wished to free her from it. What ignominy for us, and what need we have to save ourselves.

As outer action can have bad consequences for us, we have tended to forego action. There is of course the action that takes place within ourselves, and brings about a change because we have changed, but this is to recommend that a woman should be as wise as a sage. She sometimes is, from necessity, but if it is beyond her then she acts indirectly as the only way open to her, and is then told that it is a woman's nature to be indirect. So nature confines us and holds us within a circle; and if we remain there we are able to accomplish much, but we seem to step outside the circle at our peril until the problem of containment can become one of our most subtle troubles. It is so difficult to solve yet so urgent that we wonder if we ourselves can create a circle to contain ourselves: for countless women are not contained in families or in relationships, and we blow about like grains of sand.

When we are asked what women have contributed to the body or spirit of civilization, there is nothing solid we can claim as ours. We know that the great people are almost all men. Admirable women have been legion, but very few have been great. It is usually men who are creative, but seldom women. Many men have lived their heights without women, so that we cannot even say that men and women always need each other to be at their best. They do need each other to be at their most complete, and the relationship between men and women is the completeness at the core of life.

There is even a special intensity derived from living without each other, from living one's wholeness in oneself. Many great men have possessed their own feminine qualities, and many women—some nuns and some nurses —are so alive, so loving, so fulfilled, that they seem to have had no need of men. The few women who have had some greatness have generally been unmarried. Elizabeth I, Joan of Arc, Teresa of Avila, Florence Nightingale—so few over the centuries—lived their lives with a passion that required both sides of their nature. So one has to believe that there is one kind of wholeness which comes from being unrelated.

We are told that woman domesticated man, and that the bond between man and woman was the basis of culture, so our contribution has been real. We sometimes feel like saying that man is our creation, but we can be abashed by what we have done, and forego this claim. We do say that we are the inner spirit of man, and we could say that we influence him when he is most unprotected. It would be true to say that we are his most personal side, and what we are he is in his heart, so that our inferiority is of paramount importance to him. If we are man's disregarded self then our inferiority is his shame. It is even possible that man can go no further forward until we advance, with his agreement.

He wants us as the wall at his back, as his scapegoat, his delight, and his odd-job man, but he finds it almost impossible to see each of us as a person. We are said to stand in his blind spot, so we must look at ourselves, difficult as this is for us. We do it for his sake as well as for our own.

We can truly say that we have carried his shadow, lived his ideal for him and with him, and that we have prevented his seeing himself when he could not have borne it. Man inherits much of his nature from us: his compassion, his belief in tenderness, and his knowledge of love come through us. Much of his creativity comes from his own feminine side. We inherit many of our qualities from him, some of them needing attention by the time they reach us, and others the very bones of sense. We are clearly an interchange of qualities forever necessary to each other, so where does the dissonance lie? Does it even exist? Yes, that has to be admitted. There is a rift, a source of strife, something painful lies between man and woman.

All miasmas drift away when a man and a woman are content together, for when women are loved they lose their deep brand of inferiority, and gain value almost beyond their deserts; but that they are branded is one of the things that can make love uneasy. There is often a third person present in the mind of the woman, a person who is watchful and wary; who thinks that if women are considered inferior then the judgment also applies to love and to intimacy. To say that the heart of living is inferior is a great affront to life itself, and it remains a troubling mystery to women.

Because of these many things we are bound to feel that for us to be considered inferior is as bad for men as it is for women, and that for both our sakes it should end. We do not want men to come down any lower, so we must make our inferiority less true than it is at present. Which means that we must look at it again and again until we are sure what our real inferiorities are, and which we carry wrongfully. We may carry some for life's sake, and these we must keep.

Man has gone ahead of us, and is our natural leader in the outside world, as we are his support in private worlds. All that is clear. We have always been the personal side of life while man was the outer side, the side that showed and was recorded. But to be personal is not to say what qualities we possess, nor what virtues and vices are ours. We should not be compared to men, indeed it should not be possible. Men are easy to measure and there are rules to assess their value, but women are only assessed by preferences and prejudices. It is some comfort to us to know that within our own circle of rightness we are sometimes acclaimed.

It can seem that men need us to be inferior, or are we wrong, and do they only want to keep us within their pact with them, and sometimes do it clumsily in the one way that drives us out? If it is both, and they do need to feel that we are inferior, then how inferior? Could the amount be somewhat reduced? Now, after all we've done for them—surely.

Perhaps modern woman is impelled to her present behavior by a need to know who she is apart from man. We have been too tightly merged for comfort. We carried the shames of the body as though it was our fault that bodies existed, and we are impatient of this. We are tired of being man's whipping boy, for if he can call us childish, instinctive, amorphous, and unreasonable he knows where these qualities are and need not look for them in himself.

The charge of inferiority that man makes against us has been so persistent all through time that it must have deep meaning. Women are not said to be human beings with faults, as men also might be described; women are charged with the major fault of being women. As though our faults were inherent in us, and this we have found very hard.

Men say—enough that is to allow the generalization—that men must be masters of women. That is an embarrassing statement to read, but it can be found even in the writings of a modern philosopher and it is certainly found in the wishes of many men and of many women. Must we believe that men of high civilization believe in slavery? Slavery condemned and almost ended everywhere, yet deeply rooted and enjoyed in the heart of love! How we amaze ourselves! But here we are close to the realm of passion, and thought need not try to enter here. Anything may be true, and when passion masters us and we live without thought, helpless and driven, abased and exalted, men may well want to master this. So they master women in lieu of mastering themselves; an easy solution surely.

Women have always been expected to abandon themselves. This is the other side of the mastery. Abandonment is the one quality in which they have had a thorough training. They have given over their wills, their bodies, and their power of individual judgment. They could not do otherwise, but it has not happened without a deep desire for power forming in them as just compensation. And it shows where tyranny is most cruel, in close relationship.

The truth seems to be that woman likes to master, too, and that passion and abandonment give her her chance. Woman can render men so helpless here, that it is here she knows her strength and uses it as men do, without pity. If the most intense union can be the keenest strife, then the man does need his strength, and it is clear why he insists he must be master.

Warfare or peace, it can be either between men and women, and such extremes are difficult to represent truly, as well as being difficult to endure. But in our ordinary, bewildering everyday way, an individual woman is just someone struggling to understand and to live her life, wanting help and not dominion on either side. Women are tired of being the means by which men avoid knowing themselves, and if we are thought of as inferior but mastered, we have helped man to surmount himself and then forget that it was necessary; this makes us ashamed of him and of ourselves.

Of course it can be other than this, and better, and

easier. It can be anything in this game of seeing our faults in the other, and accusing the other but seldom oneself. Men know helplessness as well as women, and feeling poor they can say: "She is mine, so I am rich and trusted to be strong." So he masters his own weakness. These dramas that men and women play are secret, and women will always be partly secret. Such dramas are a desperate game of giving value, and taking value away. The marks of this passionate contest are on both, though with the deepest wounds on the woman one imagines. Well—a wounded person is always a little incalculable, even a little dangerous. Women are trying to cleanse some of their wounds now, and countless women would deny that they still existed, indeed would laugh at them as sick fancies. Yet the hurt has been given, and there is little doubt that it has its share in our turning toward a more masculine way of life.

Just because we represent the hidden side of life, we know that hidden things can fester, and because we also represent the sacred, we have a concern for our uncleanness. Men belittled us to make their masculinity dependable. We paid for their gain and perhaps life paid, too. When men belittle us they belittle half of life, and they belittle their own happiness. To demean women is to demean love and relationship, and these are the two qualities in which civilization is very weak, and which it greatly needs.

We are aware that our inferiority is partly the danger of the inchoate, we know that we carry the shadow of the unconscious with its great good and bad; it is true that the intensity between men and women is great because the woman unites man with his creative soul; we accept that behind us are great depths inimical to man as he struggles toward consciousness. We agree that the darkness of all this lies on us, we take this as true, and we ask: "Is this woman's role?"

It may be nothing less than the truth that we represent creation and destruction, and that life needs us to be nothing other than this. That would make our attempt to exist apart from man paltry and unimportant. Are we truly fated to a fluid living of someone else, always undifferentiated for their sake? It seems almost unbearable. Yet if it is true, or half true as is our way, must we not become ourselves, truly ourselves, so that we can endure foregoing ourselves so often, so that we may carry our great role, and that nothing we do may make us untrue to it? Is this our answer, found if not liked, yet meant to be lived?

Though man can do without woman, must do without her, is almost not man but still child if he cannot do without her, it is equally true to say that if he does not turn to the woman again and again he is lost in his one-sided development, and in what can be his own sterility. While if he does not turn and form a whole with the feminine side of his own nature he is lost in very truth, cut off from his own enriching and renewing sources. So part of woman's task is to represent to men what they must leave but return to. We are the symbol of their wholeness and of their humanity. We are the life that saves them from their thought, and that they must have the power to forego. This is another aspect of our being, and not being.

But does no one see, is it not obvious and even flagrant, that there are many times when we are alone, when we are not existing for anyone, not wanted to, and that then we are sharply present for ourselves, urgently needed by ourselves? And what if we are nothing then? When man is withdrawn into his own half of life we must possess ourselves in very truth. Because we are so often cut off from the life we receive from men we are forced to turn to the man in our own nature in order to give meaning to life. Since the First World War there have been millions of women living without men, and where could they look for strength to live by?

Women who live alone are forced to summon every power lying in their natures in order to survive, but this problem of what a woman shall do and be when she is not in relation to a man, concerns all women. It is a constant problem for the wife of a busy man; and the frequent waiting, the idleness, the blankness, the not doing because the husband's position requires it that are asked of many wives, require immeasurable courage and wisdom. Women who live in relationship and by it, as well as those who lack it, exist and exist sentiently when men are absent.

One could say that women must possess themselves for the sake of men. Let us say just that, for women are attempting such new things that they need the best aegis under which to shelter. For otherwise there is a great possibility of their going forward by themselves, and for themselves.

Have we not stumbled on the impious thing in woman's search for consciousness? It is—is it not—that she may seek it for herself. Is this the signpost to heed? Does it perhaps tell her that she must remain at the point where her heart is open to others. This true—nothing else matters, she can be everything; this untrue—nothing else is good. Now it almost seems that we have found the danger in our modern way, and that we can separate its good from its bad. We are tempted to a Lilith-like role of opposition, against man and against the child. It is even possible to see a likeness between our present impetus and Rossetti's strange poem "Eden Bower," in which Lilith begs the Serpent to let her take his place that she may tempt Eve.

The renegade in us could make us tempt ourselves to use consciousness for ourselves, for our own pride and our own power, and to heal old hurts. One feels the leap of truth here, but if we realize it, if this is one of the truths we must know about ourselves, then we must hope that we will choose to prevent its happening. A part of us wants to be loyal, our hearts open—though rightly closed on occasion —agreeing to redeem what needs redeeming, agreeing to be inferior where we clearly are, and when man needs to be superior, but both claiming and meriting honor for our side of life.

It is only honorable to mention that we may not be so agreeable to live with as we drop our inferiority. Stimulating perhaps, but not restful, and seldom soothing. We would be less prone to live by the expectations of others. Yet, if less agreeable, think what a gain in honesty! But honesty is not really liked in women, indeed nothing is simple where women are concerned, and to advocate consciousness in women may be ill-advised.

So perhaps it is better to point out that the fat is already in the fire. Perhaps the initial mistake was in educating women, and that mistake has already been made. There is the added disadvantage that having taken naturally to education, she has already learned too much to live the feminine myth as she has done hitherto. She will continue to play it, but she may have found a new way to play it badly, ignoring its wells of truth, and failing to see the great heart it requires of her. Or—if time is kind—she may find herself, and carry the feminine role aware of its dangers, but undaunted because of the new security she has found in herself.

Her eyes are already sufficiently open to see what resembles a pretense that entangles her. It feels like a masculine illusion—though this is doubtless one of her many illusions about men—and it makes her doubt the entire ordered fabric of life, so that she sometimes wonders if order concerns her. She has studied what religion and literature have explained that she is, and though these old precepts are changing rapidly, they are still the very warp of society's assumptions regarding women, and they greatly affect her attitude toward herself. She disagrees with many; even disagreeing profoundly, and she feels that she is something other, something more than she is said to be, and that an essential truth has been left unstated. Her thought has only recently become clear enough to make her sure that man's thought expresses but one aspect of life.

She is increasingly conscious of a marked duality in life, and she sees that men and women are drawing apart, perhaps must draw apart, in order to see each other as they are in themselves, and above all to see the other in themselves. This may well help them to see anew, and with some degree of clarity and charity, the chaos each projects on to the other. Something in woman flames, and let us hope that it is her care for human happiness, as she says to her partner, near or far "Admit that you want me to live you. If you feel that we are one, and that one is you, let us say so. If I have begun to fight for that great privilege tell me so. If we are rightly two, let us say that, and let me find out who I am. Then if we enter into a relationship, let us admit how difficult it is, requiring the effort of both, and that do what we will it is dangerous to both."

It begins to look as though the part of the feminine myth that women can no longer live is the assumption that they live entirely for men. Remembering every minute how astonishing this idea may be to men, but knowing women feel that somewhere the assumption exists and is acted on. Women grant that it is half true, but they deny that it is wholly true. What is true is love, that world of a word, for that they stand. In the transports of love and in the trials of love it is true that each is the other, but this is not true for either all the time; and we behave foolishly when we delude ourselves about this.

We are wanted to represent love and union in this striving world, but no one wants a woman to be loving all the time, so it is nonsense to suppose it. Nor—more is the pity—are all women wanted to love. The truth is that we are often not wanted, and hardly seen; we may merely represent a disregarded thing, so we are obliged to take ourselves on. Then as we become absorbed in this search for what we are, we turn to each other, ruefully at first, expecting to be bored; but no, it is all right.

In discovering ourselves we discover that we have much to say to other women, and that we say it sharply and pungently. Our talk may take surprising leaps, but it is very close to life. We find we need each other to test the validity of our new ways. We have been brought up to believe that our biological qualities must be ever present. We were to lure, yield, endure, and give succor; if we did less or other than these we were no longer women. But now when modern women have interesting work to discuss with each other they find that they do not have to behave in a biological manner, and the gaiety and honesty is delicious. This exhilarating release makes them forget that they are women, and they feel so untroubled and free that they even wonder if for the moment they have ceased to be women. That need not be decided, though the probability is that we are always women, and it is only that with the concept enlarged we enjoy having a little more room.

As for our inferiority—and now women are strong enough to look at it—we begin to wonder if it is not very real, and very precious. If we deny our inferiority we may obscure something of profound importance. Is it not perhaps true that our inferiority is an inferiority in life itself, up till now unregarded? Are we not a side of life, a way of life not yet developed or assessed truly, indeed not possible to develop until the masculine way had reached a point where it felt the lack of a way different from its own?

9

The Figure Behind Women

WHEN women fulfill their role of devotion they are granted great value, but when not in a close personal relation they have always tended to lose value in the eyes of society and in their own eyes as well. Alone they can become almost invisible and beside man they may hardly exist. As the man has usually maintained the outward position it has been practical for the woman to be his helpmate and handmaid; but great extremes of masculine egotism and feminine selflessness have been reached. A medical report on cooking pots stated that the iron pot had had certain advantages, as when there was insufficient food the mother served her husband first, then the children, and scraped the pot for herself, thus obtaining a certain amount of iron. With enamel and aluminum pots this advantage was not available.

One father of a family made his grown-up children go to their bedrooms when he wished to retire so that he could put out the drawing-room lights himself. He always put out his own bedroom light as he got into bed, leaving his wife to manage in the dark as best she could. One night it occurred to him that the rest of his family might be reading in their own rooms. He then planned to have a master switch installed in his room so that when he put out his light the entire house would be in darkness.

So the masculine role can do strange things to a man, and a woman's abnegation may be part cause of his nonsense; her harmful, helpful, exquisite abnegation; her skill in hiding behind a mask so that her husband's private life may not show, her foregoing her own preference so that she may serve the preference that is more creative than hers, her gift of remaining still so that her child may find his own daring, her quiet that allows the word spoken to her to ring with its true meaning.

All this has been our strange fate. It can of course be wholly satisfying to live for others and in others, but it is confusing to disappear. To be nothing has as marked an effect on the character as to exist. Though it has become obvious that the very essence of the feminine principle is to experience depth of being and not being, the contrast is admittedly great, and the effect on the individual can be contradictory.

All will agree that in the past women have known their fullest humanity in relationship. They have known love, selflessness, and even self-sacrifice. These high virtues were sometimes ours, and can be called our strength. But our worst side has also been an aspect of selflessness. It was the lack of a self, the lack of a point of view, the lack of an integrated ego; all of this together creating an indifference as to definitions, as though they barely existed or it mattered little when they did. Many of us having a genius for inaccuracy, women can live in what amounts to a haze of inattention about all that does not concern an individual person. People are real to them, but little else. They flow into people, into many people, and lose themselves there. Women make themselves into mirrors for others, sometimes flattering and sometimes distorting mirrors. They can be utterly formless unless someone gives them a mold to fill. Our good and our bad are so close together that it is difficult to say when a woman is at her best or her worst. One is often uncertain whether to feel awe or despair.

If we are wanted to live for others, then—delighted to be on the right road—we give our all, and naturally we have nothing left. Seldom wanted or permitted to be ourselves, always enjoined to be someone else, we do as we are asked and vanish, into someone else, of course. The advantages and disadvantages of this are many, and so it is a very great change that women are now becoming more definitely themselves.

Yet our new independence is something of an illusion, just as it was never wholly true that we were wholly dependent. Many of us are now free to make our own decisions and free to take the consequences. This excites those who are not free, and all become impatient of the deep claim that life makes on women. We become certain that we need be a problem no longer, that we are in fact solved at last. There is such a general insistence that being a woman is now a simple matter, that it must mean we forget that a woman has one foot chained by nature, so it is forever her role to dance in fetters.

Living for others may well have accumulated much un-lived and unadmitted selfishness in us, so that now when we live in our own right we can be driven by an almost ravening need. It could hardly be otherwise. To be harsh, to be downright, to be indifferent even, is liberating. To be unfeeling is almost the new honesty. And it may take women some time to feel clean of the too personal.

As woman's participation in life so often entails an extreme of selfless giving, one might suppose she would always have been greatly honored; and—as there was real danger of her losing herself—that she would have been warned. If we could look at it with fresh eyes we would expect that common caution would make a deep awareness of her innate duality the chief thing taught to women. But that is not at all how it has been. No garnered wisdom has said to women: "As you will give—make sure that you give from fullness; otherwise you are flotsam and cling from emptiness. As you will have to accept, and will sometimes receive what repels you, be sure you create clear values, so that your 'Yes' and your 'No' both protect life. As you are bound to know helplessness, be steadfast. As you will have to conform, have a value in your own heart to which you can always be true."

It was, of course, for women to find the words that they needed, and if we have not done so it is our failure. I think we have failed to garner wisdom for ourselves. Instead we have listened to society, and what society seemed

to say was something like this: "You don't belong to yourselves, but to others. It is the claim of others that will decide your lives. So forget yourselves, and try to be what
others want you to be."

That is startling advice to receive, and it has had some
dubious consequences. At some deep level in us we are still
amazed and still saying: "Really forget ourselves? Is that
safe? Isn't it an alibi for everything? If we lose ourselves
what will we have, and for whom are we to be so malle-
able? Can we trust them? Does anyone know what
they're asking of us?"

It was advice that had to be followed, and if we have
adapted ourselves until we are instinctive chameleons, no
one can complain. If for centuries society has confused us,
and we have shown much sense and some irony by be-
having as well as we sometimes do, we now have greater
need of clarity than ever before. For we are strongly
tempted to take a new line that may destroy much good,
and we are also becoming capable of the creation of that
exquisite thing, a true balance. A balance in ourselves.
This is a possibility that deserves every help, for it is not
yet a certainty. We may decide that we do not want a balance, a difficult thing entailing insight, honesty, and love.
We may prefer to rebel against our paradoxical role, and
we may live our rebellion against the difficulty of being
a woman. Many seem to be out of patience with it, or is it
truer to say that we need the exhilaration of a respite?

Many are attempting to live devotion and freedom at
the same time. Conscientious as ever, we give ourselves
and we withhold ourselves; day by day and hour by hour

we attempt to balance the two, but we have not yet found the correct amount of either. We know that woman will always live many forms of acceptance. We see that all about us, and know it in ourselves.

We are often helpless, our fundamental position is one of inherent helplessness. The kind of child a woman bears is almost outside her control. The ability and quality of her husband decides her place in society, and his prestige is her prestige. So everything says that to receive is a large part of woman's role. But this a very big role. It matters who receives, and whether they honor or misuse the thing given them. If you accept you also contain, and your influence is beyond measure. It has been very reckless of society not to take woman more seriously, for it needed the best of her, and it often engendered the worst.

Let us look at the effect of some of society's expectations of woman, following some of the paths by which she loses herself, or finds herself. She so often combines the two that perhaps society should be exonerated for its cynical and pragmatical attitude toward her. Since time began men have tried to fit women into men's requirements, and into the pattern of society that men of necessity have been forming. Women have tried to be as men wished, and needed them to be. But to live by adaptation to others can have a disintegrating effect on the character, so women have been coaxed and cosseted into thinking about themselves as little as possible.

Adapting to others can make you very aware, as you slowly understand who you are supposed to be. You accept the form given you, but you know where it doesn't fit, and where it does not belong to you, but belongs more to the giver. So acceptance creates a doubt, it may be the source of woman's double vision, and also of her irresponsibility; as though she feels that the laws she lives under do not make sense. Her role of acceptance has caused her to mock at the simplicity of men who asked her to play a game of make-believe, and then believed it themselves.

For it felt to her as though she was told not to be honest. She must pretend that she was an empty vessel; she must hold man's passion, his joy, and often his sorrow. Also his hate and his scorn. She must hold what she was given. She must hold her own emptiness as well, for her being empty seemed of her very essence. But emptiness can be hard to endure and it has an annihilating effect, as though emptiness increases emptiness.

But this was only half the truth, for woman had to give. She was also a full vessel, a vessel that gave and gave and must never run dry. A vessel that gave food and comfort, agreement and support. A mute vessel that could not refuse what was put into it, or taken out of it; bad might be wanted from it as well as good. And the vessel was continually told that it was its nature to accept and to give, that it was being untrue to its nature if it did either more or less.

No one can say that this picture is true of any one woman, but many women would recognize in it one aspect of the feminine principle. It may approximate a little to what society has asked woman to be and it may also tell us why she has evaded and railed at her role. Being a vessel is like everything feminine, it is both painful and pleasurable. Every woman protests at some aspects of it, and some women have protested with all their might and main. The protests were discordant and unwelcome, but they did some good, for each protest reminded women, and society, that women are not entirely feminine, but partly masculine.

The masculine in us ponders over the contrast between the masculine and feminine principles, and the polarity between them. If men define, make hard and clear, then ceaselessly fight that the definitions of each may prevail, is it not perhaps necessary that the opposite of this must exist too, must be maintained and lived by the other half of life? Oneness must exist as well as division, peace as well as war, agreement as well as difference, giving as well as taking; there must be ease to balance effort, comfort to ease combat, and unprotesting oneness to balance all that man does and is.

If acquiescence was needed, and one sees the greatness of the balance involved, should it not have been honored? Sometimes it was, and we had best put aside the whole question of honor, for our acquiescence must often have been blankness, and unfit for honor; and so often quiescence led to happiness. Have we drawn near to a great truth here, and can we say that what women were living was containment and receptivity, and this was a vital good, though often lived blindly? The individual woman has to separate herself from it to see what she has been serving, but it is most possible that she has been representing an essential virtue.

If the feminine principle represents oneness, is that not

the great value of which we are much in need? Is it not the value that is now recognized in thought, in morals, worked for by politicians, as well as lived blindly on lower levels? Has the world reached an extreme in its knowledge of division, until its hope of salvation lies in oneness, until oneness is the emergent principle among us, and has indeed become the world's concern?

It could be said that oneness is not the same as emptiness, or not being, which is the aspect of the feminine we have been considering. That is true, yet if not being is the demeaned half of oneness that women have lived, it becomes more easily understood when seen as a part of oneness. Emptiness is needed that fullness may give it itself. Emptiness is required that its opposite may appear, since the non-insistent allows the insistent to declare itself, and even stop insisting so much. These intangibles are very difficult to make clear, but no one can deny their existence or importance. If women have lived emptiness and not being, and women are newly in the ascendant, are they bringing the good of their quality into equal prominence? Receptivity that sees what it accepts, remaining clear-eyed as to what is good and what is bad, is almost an inner reasonableness; and it is the quality that resolves combat. Is it any wonder that life has insisted it should be represented somehow, even in the uncomfortable terms known to women, since the virtues inherent in it are perhaps yet to be fully explored?

As life battered at women, belittled and belied them, what was life saying? That men must fight with their minds and their skills and their force, but that their way of life needed our way of life as safe balance, and must not fight it, that being the sin which brings shame on us both. Was life saying that weakness existed to let strength know its own good and its bad? It might be said that strength needed weakness to learn what it must not do, and women were that weakness. Strength also needed weakness to cherish and pity and we were that weakness as well.

But now women do not want to be weak, insist on being strong, and they often prove themselves so strong that it has the result of making everyone around them weak. On occasion they must know all and do all, and carry all the weight there is. They can expend themselves until they almost breathe for their families, and when they are truly spent they can keep the home circle in bondage by heart attacks, timed to have the greatest disciplinary effect. Because we begin to see the harm we do to ourselves and to others by living our strength with blind determination, because we can at last think almost clearly, and are on the verge of observing ourselves, we see that strength can do harm, and that there is great virtue in our receptive role, essential virtue that we have had to rediscover for ourselves.

Women have almost reached a point where they understand the feminine principle, see what it stands for, and what it is that women represent. They may even begin to understand what men have wanted them to hold fast to. It is quite possible that this discussion is not about the individual woman, but about the many-sided archetype that stands behind woman, terrifying and fructifying to men and women alike. If we can understand her then women might begin to win for themselves an ideal to live by; and as its heights and its depths would be great, it might become clear that only a conscious and many-sided human being could hope to live so difficult and important an aspect of life.

Can we catch the glimpse we have had in a statement like this: "Behind the individual woman is a figure of essential femininity who is being, not doing, forgiveness, not force; who gives and so is to some degree selfless; who gives knowing the gift may be too much, but trusting the recipient to render the gift harmless. A figure who receives and has to make the gift fruitful; who effaces herself and yet is reality, and the challenge of reality; who exists though unrecognized, whose quality is love, and the spring of life. Who can neither protest not insist, or she is not herself. Who is trusted not to be the other side of herself, and so must constantly consume and transmute the other side. This means she must somehow transmute the desirous and destructive, the inchoate and volcanic, both in herself and in others. She is herself a denial of these things which are yet always present in her. When she can receive and clarify them she has peace to offer. She is a figure whose good makes evil safe, and so she is completeness."

Thus outlined she proves not to be at all mysterious, but familiar to us all, and lived by every woman when at her most natural.

10

The Outer Scene

I T hardly makes sense to look at women without looking more closely at their modern background. When we do that it becomes clear that the same qualities of wholeness, and undifferentiated relationship for which women have always stood, are dominant in society, one might say in the world at large. As one would expect, they are present both in their good and bad. Humbled at the daring of making so large a generalization, one yet suggests that wholeness and division are the two dominant issues in the world today. So that women in their new division and their innate wholeness are living, almost representing the qualities of these extraordinary times.

We experience division politically in the mutual fear of East and West. The atom has been split, and this is division of such power that man recoils from his own act. Now he knows his own power of destruction and can hardly know worse of himself. It may be that our fear of ourselves dominates us, and drives us together. There is a general fear of having definite outlines, and of being responsible for one's individual difference. The tendency among us to obliterate all lines of demarcation is strong and many sided. The query of "Why not?" is heard on all sides. "Why shouldn't men and women be alike?" "Why is sexual perversion not as good as normal sexuality?" "Why can't we all be alike?" This desire to merge has a large element of fear behind it, as though differences bring conflict, and the ultimate conflict of war is so terrible, that we want to be all one, all safe, hence there must be little difference between us.

Every effort of reason and good will goes into forming pacts, and strengthening bonds that will hold nations in union, and thus further safety. Political beliefs, morality, and even manners say with different voices that we must all join. Any form of exclusiveness seems displeasing to prevailing taste; we must not refuse anyone or anything. We must accept all, as though all were alike. This attitude is so general that we feel its insistent imposition from outside, and its burgeoning in our own hearts. Exclusiveness has had a long reign, but it has apparently lived its full span, and inclusiveness now appears to offer the needed thing.

We are so abashed to have what others lack, that there is even a show of confusion at being definitely yourself; as though to be markedly individual might appear exclusive, and all are quick to deny any such claim. The new courtesy lies in softening your outlines as much as possible, in seeming to melt into everyone else, in being so tolerant that definition fades. Tolerance is the prevalent virtue, and tolerance tells us that it is kinder to see sameness, not difference. To be the same is the new fellowship, and the old human tendency to try to be more than you were, or to pretend to be more than you are, is displaced by a haste to disclaim all that you are and have.

Compassion is half cause of much of our behavior, and compassion is perhaps the greatest virtue of inclusiveness. It is so basic a good, so near to insight, so close to love, that one is ashamed not to accept acceptance without a second glance. Yet something that we all experience warns us that a second glance is necessary. Try as we may we cannot fail to see that if inclusiveness increases good will, thus making a warmer humanity, it also creates the amorphous. This is its bad as compassion is its good. The formless, the meaningless, and the tasteless are the dangerous aspects of our new ideal.

We seem to be under a compulsion to include the lowest point, and this may have profound meaning. There is a marked tendency to make the weakest sacrosanct. Our present stress on the importance of the weak might once have been called diseugenic, as strength and ability were considered desirable; but now we are hardly interested in strength, and instead we thrill with a sense of emotional enrichment when we can include the problematic, and improve slightly the almost hopeless. As this attitude is strong and insistent, necessity may dictate it, and health may lie in it. Self-preservation may even be its cause. Our position may be so perilous that weak spots are grave threats. But it impresses the imagination as having further meaning, for it has every appearance of being part of a persistent, though unconscious, search for wholeness.

Wholeness in a political sense appeared in the dictatorships that sprang up in many countries just before and after the First World War. The Fascist movement, the Nazi movement, communism, these were all imposed forms of wholeness; violent, spontaneous events that engulfed individuals without their understanding what had happened. Within these movements the individual became helpless while the reign became all powerful. Imposed wholeness had arrived, had to be accepted, and the individual found himself much less of a person than he had been before.

Strangely enough, another and very different form of wholeness appeared somewhat earlier. The treatment of mentally disturbed people showed that the human psyche must be regarded as including the unconscious as well as the conscious. Later this inclusion proved to be so far-reaching in its meaning, so numinous in character that it may prove to be the birth of a new morality, even a new vision of God.

The morality that a psychological attitude entails is based on the inclusion of all one's disparate parts, so that here, too, the inclusion of the lowest point is implicit. In the psychological discipline that has resulted, the necessity of becoming responsible for your shortcomings, and for your sins, takes first place. This amounts to enduring the conflict of good and evil within yourself; which is of course an acceptance of the tension of opposition in all things. The aim of this treasured but painful experience is that the individual may be faithful to his individual way, receiving the fecundation of the unconscious as a spiritual responsibility. This is inclusiveness of a searing and healing kind; necessitating great self-discipline, but also bringing conviction of life's greatness.

It is a curious and arresting thing that the inclusion of discordant parts is being lived in so many ways. The mass way and the individual way, the blind way and the conscious way. The collective way can be a dictatorship, or it can achieve a welfare state. In every form the weak are included, and in the collective form there is the odd result that everyone takes on a new helplessness. In the individual way—when it is creative—the individual contains his own weak side, and the containing order is found in the laws of his own being. These two forms of inclusiveness are both part of our modern life. They express the very flavor of the age. It could be surmised that as crowd values rise to completeness the integration of the individual comes as necessary safeguard; also as possible forerunner of the value of the future; for what is more likely than that democracy having raised the level of the whole, the individual may then rise to new heights.

There is a third form of inclusion which we live half unknowingly. Our thoughts, our manners, and our preferences voice it. It is seen in our need of others. Two wars with casualties in the millions, and cruelties of a barbaric kind, are enough to make us all humble, disillusioned, and full of self-doubt. Small wonder that it is the social idiom of the time to declare one's bankruptcy— as though we draw together to share our guilt. And we have grave reasons for a sense of shame, both because of what has happened, and for fear of what may.

It would be profoundly realistic, and it would show deep moral responsibility, if we felt that world events had been so cataclysmic that humanity must look to its quality, and so must we. But it is not a serious and fateful cry of "Mercy on me" of which I write, but of a more guileless openness, almost a moral undress. We prattle of our failings until it resembles a widespread need to declare all, that all may be forgiven. Brightly, frivolously, we practice self-abasement as though driven to let others know how little they may expect of us. At its worst it can sound like a declaration that one has reached one's lowest point, and means to stay there. But is it not also a moving declaration of a need to be honest, and to have one's nothingness accepted?

This obsessive humility may hold a seed of good. If we are impelled to announce in countless ways that we are nothing, is it weakness, despair, or just true? What word will state it for what it is? It is certainly a collective intimacy, a desire to have all barriers down, all weakness known, as though this alone would permit nearness to one's brother, and nearness were the chief thing sought.

This thirst to be included, this urge to be at one with others, is it only a flight to reach the common denominator that we may know where we are, or is it a need to lose ourselves? Is it so intolerable to carry one's own uniqueness? Or are we hearing a plea that no one must differ, that no one must insist upon difficult standards and virtues, since if these were to separate us from our fellows it were better not to have them? It may be just this, but it may well be more.

Undubitably it is wholeness that is craved, and of a kind that is partly to be dreaded. It is imposed on us all to some extent, for its very existence infects us. It entails the disparagement of the individual that the strength and rightness of the crowd may be felt; and what is this but the wholeness of the all-containing tribe, which has represented safety for aeons of time? It seems like a panic rout toward anonymity, a fear of the individuality that is beyond us, a blind hunger for a oneness that we can all share. But if it is new life appearing in an undifferentiated way it is important how we receive it.

The dictated wholeness that was tried in some countries and discarded with relief, still continuing in dubious form in other countries, might have frightened anyone, yet humanity continues to make itself uniform. If we do it to ourselves even when it is not done to us then unanimity must be what we want, for good or bad reasons.

The regression into the crowd could be a dissolution of individual values, or it could be a new merging that might bring rewards. This mass tendency is developing just at a time when a minority are in search of their individual being, seeking and finding the kingdom within them, so the two tendencies make one wonder if society will split into an elite, and a proletariat of those who wish to be released from the burden of being individuals. This would be a strange result of our search for equality.

Inscrutable as it all is, certain things are clear. Wholeness includes evil as well as good, and this can result in a vagueness as to which is which, even an indifference as to which is which, so all standards become lower. But wholeness entails a new attitude toward evil. We have had such experience of evil during the recurrent wars, that a sick recoil from it might have seemed likely, a new search for good might have been expected.

This new search exists and shows clearly, but so does the predominating fascination of evil. Crime fiction is part of general reading, films of violence and bestiality are our chosen diversion. We cannot have enough of our own unpleasantness. Looked at from this angle discrimination has gone; we have chosen our worst side, bathe in its mire, and this being true is it any wonder that we despair of ourselves?

And yet hope rises immediately because of the nobility and courageous reality of countless human beings. And is their fineness not shown by their willingness and their ability to hold evil close to good, matching fear with courage, and sin with humility? Indeed what is good but that which remains undismayed in the face of evil, even balancing the two, carrying them until they are seen to belong together, and perhaps transcending them by acceptance. If in the individual the conscious carrying of this eternal conflict is strength and wisdom, if going beyond good and evil is the goal of the rare few, then there is a resemblance between this and our modern love of inclusion that can only arrest criticism and make judgment uncertain.

Even our blind inclusion shows much insight and compassion. If these qualities seem too great to be truly descriptive of our present ways, and often they do seem so, yet it could still be true to say that the amorphous and the chaotic are at least the dark side of oneness. They are not the balance of understanding, or the acceptance that love and pity can encompass, but they do resemble them. If there is any likeness at all between them, then perhaps some vital truth is being spoken with many voices, and though at times we feel nothing but bewilderment and distaste, we may be in the presence of something holy, though rudimentary because long neglected.

Hesitatingly I suggest that at this very time when intellects tell us that the Christian era is over, that it is now the heart gropes toward living it. Perhaps we only do it at our lowest point, but does that perhaps warrant a surmise that as we have for long tried to do without the wholeness that is God, our need may now express itself blunderingly in a cry of "We are one."

11

Devotion

WOMAN has always given value to the individual; her passionate belief in the uniqueness of one person almost amounting to her dominant characteristic. Now that individuals are in danger of being lost in the mass, there is great need of this feminine quality. So let us look at devotion, face some of its aspects, and note some of its results.

It is often said that women exist for the happiness of men and of children. Any woman's heart leaps at the thought of being cause of happiness, but then her heart may slow a little as she finds that she is neither simple enough nor good enough to accept this wholeheartedly. Her grudging spirit or her realism give warning, and she recognizes that to live in order to make others happy is her old fate of living for others; which may be her true and right role, but which dismays her, and with some cause. Back comes her old sense of being effaced, and with it come grave doubts about this great task of making another person happy. To love someone so that it makes him happy, but what a commitment that is! If love is as severe a test as this, and it usually is, then of course she pauses.

She gives love, but the recipient is the judge of whether her love has given happiness. So some part of her mocks at anyone's expecting to be made happy on his own terms, and marvels that anyone dare ask it. She also marvels that he does not see what is frequently the result of his expectation; that by giving she may make hateful the one who receives. This is a contradiction that dismays her. To make someone happy—how good it sounds—but this intention and expectation can have such surprising consequences. It is expected to succeed, and indeed it often does, and a woman is cause of happiness, and then all is solved. But—the but is a large one, and had better be examined no matter how much everyone regrets it. Happiness has a well-known elusiveness: it is more apt to be present if not sought, it is chary of being caught and in instant flight if pinned down. So as women know much of happiness, they are quite right to feel strongly about it.

Part of woman's rebellion may be her realization that happiness does harm in some of its guises. We may have taken a long time to discover this, but we are now convinced of it. Making those we love happy sounds innocent as a dove, but it can be as destructive as a lion. We may weaken and lessen the persons we love because it is what they want, or it is what we want. To be allowed to be one's least is one idea of love. It is a service to love not to think too well of it, for then we may see what we do in its name. Love is not even invariably welcome, its quality depending on the quality of the person who loves. So what we are comes first, and the value of our love follows.

Women should know all this, and much besides, but our great failure is that most of us know so little about being women. We might at least know, since we so often live it, that we give the name of love to bickering as well as to cosseting, fuss, and flattery; with virtues weakened and vices flourishing, until giving happiness may be giving blindness to a recipient who wants blindness, and is most content when at his worst. But this means that there is ignominy in love, and ugliness, so that love is dangerous. We might have been expected to garner such knowledge as this through the ages, but we have not always done so.

It is as dangerous for a woman to be expected to love as it is for a man to be expected to be strong, and when someone's happiness is given into her hands, she can feel as a man does when war is declared. Both may learn that the means did not justify the end. We have had so much experience of unhappiness in this war-riven age, that few people think of happiness as they used to. It is no longer a thing to give or receive as though either men or women were pampered children; it is no one's right any longer, but a brave exchange, precious and precarious.

Let us look further into this matter of insuring happiness, since women still stand for happiness though the form of giving changes. Happiness is what we want to give, yet seeing what the effect of love can be, we hesitate and we say: "If you want me to make you worse, I'll with-hold my love, and once held back then what—what am I to do with it?"

Our eyes are so open now, open to ourselves and to life itself, that we are uncertain and we are humble. Almost because our hearts open too easily and our minds are more awake then they used to be, we are feeling our way into a new concept of giving and we are unsure. We know the terms must be more honest. It is honesty that makes many women want to give warning that women are not partic-ularly loving. This of course may have been noticed.

We admit that we often have little idea of how to create happiness. The word frightens us somewhat and we would like to know what is meant by it, and what will be expected of us in that guise. We promise nothing, we hope that we will sometimes behave so that a reason-able person might feel his heart lighter for our presence. We would like to think that when we are unbearable, as we are sure to be, that our partner may be forebearing, and that when he is ignoble we may still be clear-eyed as to his absent good, as well as to his present bad. We pray that we will never by our smallness prevent another being all that it was in him to be, and that we may find in each other those latent riches that needed a welcome before they could appear.

As we now have a sensitive pride as to what we are in ourselves, it is quite likely to make us uncomfortable for others. We were doubtless nicer when we forgot ourselves; for pride was the quality that women abandoned in love, proud to let it go. One of the chief aspects of love is giving oneself as though one would henceforth be the other, or be as he wished. It is the esctasy of love that it is greater than reason, is indeed the great escape from reason. The man asks to be asked to perform a dangerous task the better to prove his love. The joy of ending the tension of being oneself is great. Both men and women long to lose themselves, or to find something greater than themselves, and give their being to that.

Men want to face an ultimate test of themselves, and they face it in achievement and in war. Perhaps women also want to surpass themselves, but in love. Love and courage and understanding all seem to be on the same road as the abandonment sought by mystics in the love of God, when one's being is annihilated and there is only God. The ways of love change, and they may be changing now. The love that mounts to a climax and then requires extinction may be waning. It can look as though this was a masculine form of love, built on the intensity of physical passion and the need to end it. Feminine love may be what women are striving for now, and it has—as far as it is yet clear—integration of conflict as its aim.

Love that was the sublime escape from oneself, when at last one lived, and finally one was conscious, always ended tragically. It is only half permissible to look critically at such ultimate things, yet love that was a conflagration could not help us to lead our daily lives, and we need a love that will do this, serving it as a constant creation.

Just because women fail love, and blur it and demean it, we know that if we stand for love we must find a way to integrate our mutual failings into love. We may well be sick of playing at goodness, and we are understandably replete with mock selflessness, and not being, and not knowing who we are. Because we have lived true devotion, and on rare occasions true selflessness, we seek the nerve of truth in all this, that we may find a better way.

The very word selfless has become equivocal, as it so often means nothing better than unconsciousness; and we all know that one woman's amorphous state can serve as excuse for her entire family remaining nebulous and practically unborn. Her love can hold her family in a state of mutual self-indulgence, all together, all soft, all greedy for comfort, no one wanting to step an inch into the hard world. Trouble of some sort is almost bound to come and then one member of the family finds that he can fail; and one having gained this much individuality, the rest may open their eyes.

Immaturity in mothers has such a retarding effect that educational authorities are greatly concerned. The numbers of children who refuse to go to school are rising so rapidly that psychologists have been called in to help. In the majority of cases it is found that the mother is herself childish, so tied to her own mother that she does not want the child to go to school as her loneliness would then be unbearable.

Just because true devotion can be the greatest good, only faintly glimpsed by most of us, we must stop easy pretense about it. Our selflessness is too often only an escape from self-knowledge; it is the evasion of responsibility for our qualities, and it is fear of the reality of our role. If devotion can be softening indulgence it can also require great courage when those we love need to ignore us, or need to see us clearly, or need to find their strength outside our concern. And they usually need, as a small extra, to know that we solidly and contentedly exist without them.

Once more we are back at the paradox, the point of contradiction in women, where conflicting things are true. Where it is the very pulse of her reality that she gives herself in relationship, and for the sake of relationship, must have an intense life of her own. When someone says: "Nothing is as real as our relationship? This is the best there is?" she answers: "Togetherness is the best there is."

Yet side by side with this and inherent part of it, is her need of acute self-knowledge and courageous independence. The more she loves the more she needs to exist in her own right, for the other may need to forego her, may need her not to protest or show her suffering; and may even need her to accept the fact that he lives most fully and reaches his best when he is without her.

When he goes she has to put aside the person she was with him, and she has to call up another side of herself, a side she may have denied and neglected, and may even have allowed to sink into a rough and uncultivated condition. She has an immeasurable need of the other half of her innate whole, and when she has it this can amount to a second togetherness. It is the part of her that lives by impersonal values, that is capable of being alone, and which she requires if she is to be fit to live in relationship. But she has not been trained to have this other half and she is seldom warned that it is partner to her softness and fluidity, so she may have a bitter fight before she finds it. It is possible that we have all heard too much of the romance of love and too little of its hardship and heroism.

The importance of relationship is almost a modern discovery, and of love there is seldom enough, so as these two things are the basis of the feminine principle, we will be wise to dwell on them a little longer. Are women wrong when they demur at living for others? At its best it is clearly their greatest good, their one sure merit, and true contribution. In refusing it they often make themselves less and life poorer. But can it be aimed at, or counted on? Surely not.

Yet as loving or not loving both have such serious consequences, we ought to know what we think about both these states, and perhaps we need initiation in so great a task, and certainly better preparation than we have ever had before. Perhaps part of the preparation is learning to know what women truly are, and what life wants of them.

We would have to face our own unwillingness to love, for it is in us, and we show it. Our myth of utter devotion is not true. We do not live it or attempt to understand it. But then if you have lived a dictated role your power to consider hardly exists. It is part of the individual you gave up when you began playing the role of devoted woman. So let us learn devotion in all its nuances, not forgetting our dismay at its cost, realizing that when we live for others we still exist, remembering that though we are women we often feel neither receptive nor merciful. Though we think we are living for others we still have all our dislikes, they are in us and sometimes stronger than we are; so we are always ourselves whether we know it or not, and whether those we love like it or not. It is small wonder that with our eyes more open than formerly, and in this rapidly changing world, we feel we must study our greathearted and highly disciplined role of being women.

Woman is wanted to be soft and to represent the soft side of life, but softness is part of the formlessness for which she is blamed. She cannot well be one without the other. She has needed to be excessively adaptable so that wherever her husband went she could happily follow; yet she could not possibly do this if she were not somewhat formless. She is told what her role is by nature and by society, and then she is belittled if this role necessitates her having certain qualities. These qualities are useful to society, let it be admitted, but let it also be realized that if society wants softness it gets a bad softness as well as a good softness, and a bad formlessness as well as a good one. If society could see what it asks of woman, she would not be called such harsh names.

Everyone sees and cannot help but see, the harshness in our natures. Perhaps we would not so often rasp the ears with our strident voices, and wound dependent hearts with our irrational hardness, if we had not been expected for so long to yield, to adapt, and to ape passivity when it scarcely made sense; equally often being asked to produce invincible strength when strength was needed. So let it be conceded by all that we are both soft and hard, and that both are needed and are asked for. When we are supposed to be living only the soft side of our natures the hard side is there, and the blind obstinacy of a soft, formless woman is a rock on which many a man has been wrecked.

Women are saddened and sickened by weakness in men, and men are chilled and angered by hardness in women. But we both know that these opposing things are part of us, so can we not relieve each other of any expectation that it could be otherwise? We might even ask help of each other in meeting our contradictions. Yet there may be danger here, for the consciousness we seek could make men and women more alike, could even make too conscious what is best left unconscious. Indeed any enlargement of consciousness is frightening as it can do harm, making cerebral what should spring spontaneously. For consciousness, too, is good and bad, so we can only hope to remain safe and sound if we take fresh steps cautiously, careful not to stray too far from nature. But this, too, is nonsense, knowing as we must that there is no hope of remaining safe, there is only sense in expecting danger as well as safety.

Man and woman together have always represented wholeness. The happiness and satisfaction they know together are caused by their completeness; reinforced by the other, augmented by the unknown in each, the joy and rest lie in opposites meeting with all conflict stilled. This vision lies in the soul of both men and women; a good that is somehow present even in our blundering unions, and that many men and women have won for themselves in very truth. Though even these fortunate ones would admit that their wholeness included some disillusionment and suffering, as all wholeness must.

If this wholeness is wanted, is felt to be the best there is, how are we to come nearer to it? Must we not first know our own shortcomings, and cleanse ourselves of some of our darkness? We have tended to ask the other to live our lacks for us, the woman wanting the man to be her outer strength and right action, expecting him to do all the clear thinking that was needed; while he expected her to live solace, and to contain him in a relationship that he might not see or value.

Such a balance can make a whole that may last a lifetime, but if it breaks the woman sees that the man's feeling is so rudimentary that it could not possibly understand her feeling, and the man sees that her thought is so childish that it resented the reality of his thought. So there is division where before there was wholeness. When he was thought and she was feeling they both lived their best qualities, though their poorest qualities were present. When he assesses her thought, and she judges his feeling, each appears at his lowest point and neither wants the other.

It has been through the opposite sex that we have lived our duality and known completeness in the other. For young people, and for simple people, this can be the first good and it may continue for a long time; but for many it has been broken and is no longer possible. The woman is already allied to her masculine side, and the man may have become aware of his feminine side and he wants it to develop and grow. He may have taken on his own feeling, and no longer needs the woman to live it for him in what may have been a blind and rudimentary way. The simple way has ended for many people, and they have no alternative to a conscious relationship based on an understanding of themselves.

12

How Can We Agree?

I F love is woman's right way how is she to live it? For the sad truth is that love never comes to many women, playing no part in their lives at all. They are often ill-fitted for it, are at a loss as to its true nature, so never win their greatest good nor find it in their own hearts. If love avoids some of us, it visits others only to prove us failures. For love is a thing seldom taught, known to have aspects without end, yet left to be learned as best we may. We are counted on to feel some manner of love by virtue of being women, but we fail in our commission as often as we succeed, though if we are creating a new way there is fresh ground for hope.

Everyone believes in love, and no one wholly gives over hoping for it. We read of it, await its visitation, the poets tell us that it exists. They too often imply that it casts its radiance then goes, leaving sorrow in its place, but in spite of all its dangers we envy those to whom it comes.

The comic aspects of love are forever funny. Funnier to men than to women, men tending to find bodily functions comic. It is comic to be at the mercy of one's body, though women take bodies more seriously than men; have to take bodies seriously, as the delights of the body can lead women into long responsibilities from which men are free. Women cannot regard bodies as men do, so how can they agree about love?

A man seems—to a woman—to enjoy the pleasures of the body almost more if he can forget the human being in the body. A woman may represent all the human qualities that he fails to see, and she can spend much time in saying "I am in my body," without its being heard. She also says, though less frequently: "I can't wear your ideal, for it doesn't suit me."

But if women refuse both the heights and depths that men offer them, how is it possible for the man to discover that she is the place where the two meet? The meeting of the two is perhaps what she is at last trying to bring about. This may be what she means by relationship. This covering word perhaps implies an avowal of difference, of equal need and equal honor, and a recognition of duality in each. It may also shelter mutual dislike and mutual fear, as well as a shared effort in binding heights and depths into a whole.

This whole is split into love and hate when the woman finds the man not good enough to help, for then she cannot live her devotion. When her love is great enough to encompass his bad, seeing it clearly, her strength is dearly bought but unbreakable. Her danger is of course that she may play her role of devotion by lying to herself, by playing the ancient game of make-believe where the man remains blind and she becomes meaningless.

But is honesty versus mercy not the whole test and pitfall of love? If we see clearly can we still love? It may well require a depth of compassion we lack, so that we content ourselves with the easy love of mutual pretense. Women are constantly caught in this problem of respect in love, feeling that it is intolerable to do without it, but too often finding it is their special fate to have to forego it, until they are lamed and broken by its lack.

We know that if a woman forces consciousness on her husband about these matters, it can easily seem treachery in his eyes. It can result in quarrels that are patched up by the instincts, and both may declare that they did not mean a word of what both stated with so much vigor. If the woman insists that she loves, and yet meant every uncomfortable word that she said, she can seem a monster of unnaturalness. She has appealed to her husband's power of thought which he uses elsewhere, but hopes to be relieved of when with her. She may even insist that when she refuses to be the sole caretaker of their feeling bond, that she does it in the name of love.

The woman seems impelled by the very spirit of the age to say to the man: "I exist apart from you. I have a point of view that differs from yours. We are not one but two. We cannot be truly related unless you see and admit that we are separate, as well as together." She may go deeper and say: "It is not safe for us to be together unless we realize that we are a danger to each other."

The man may very well reply that she destroys herself when she destroys their unity, as she exists to maintain it. He can add that he has enough trouble in the outer world, that if he solves it successfully then surely she can guard the bond that unites them. This can sound in her ears like the just rebuke of an injured man.

When peace has been restored between them she still knows that what she almost destroyed was his blindness. Yet she may have done harm, and if she has been caught by an idea, and it has made her sharp and mechanical, driven her crazily like an ungoverned machine, then she may have done real harm. But if she has only voiced the thought that felt true in her heart, never ceasing to care for the value that they have created together, then though she may well feel bewildered she need not feel wholly guilty.

Yet she is almost bound to ask herself: "Must men be allowed their blindness about relationship and about themselves, the two seeming to go together? And how much blindness do they need? Must woman be conscious alone in the place where he is not? She is so often blank where he is clearly defined—and as he carries the responsibility of the outer world, and often of essential work, should she not carry the strain of the personal world, understanding for both, enduring for both?"

It is here that women struggle for clarity. They plead that though they protect and indulge and support, they cannot respect blindness, and their love needs more reasons for respect than is sometimes offered. Reasons within reason. They have reached a point, perhaps they arrived there long ago, where they cannot respect a man because he is a man, or love him because they said they would and thought they could, nor because a woman should be loving.

They are now impelled to seek and create, fight and suffer for an openness where the faults of each can be admitted. Where the effect of her behavior on him and his behavior on her is seen and responsibility for it accepted; when neither expect their unlovable behavior to bring them love, but when each can include the destructive side as inherent part of the whole.

While a woman is making this effort she can give her husband cause to hate all women, and she can easily hate herself. Consciousness can feel like her worst enemy, and the disturber of all that is dearest to her. She wishes that she truly lacked a mind, but she wishes in vain, for consciousness is growing in her, and education has proved destructive of her former peace. She is aware as perhaps never before, and it is not surprising that her awareness shows in personal relations and in love. This is said without forgetting that love is thought to be blind, perhaps must be blind, and that it is love for which women stand.

Having reached this point we can only ask: "How blind must love be?" We know that a place can be reached where love is clear-sighted and yet is still love. It is not easy to reach that place and not possible to remain there long. We sometimes live there for a while before we realize that love has transcended contradiction. But those are the heights of love, and on our daily level we often love in a way that to an outside observer can look utterly blind.

As though blindness was required of women, and nothing less would enable them to magnify those they love, to cleanse them of all blemish, to regard them as the very norm of reason, and sometimes to see them as the center of the universe.

Blindness may have been given women as the one quality that allowed her to live devotion. Only this attribute could let her believe that her handicapped child was normal, and with a faith that flamed into the fanatical, helped her to bring it nearer normality. The blindness of love is not a thing to assess lightly, one can only recognize it and marvel.

If we agree that blindness has been asked of women, even to excess, then we can understand more easily the contradiction in her present position. For now life seems to ask reason of her and what amounts to detachment. These qualities in a man are sound and satisfying, but are they really wanted in women? Would a man want them applied to him? Well—it is possible, for blind devotion must have become cloying to both participants by now.

But how reasonable is it safe for a woman to be? Love and even devotion are beyond reason, outside reason, and when a woman is pledged to the well-being of her family it helps if she can see that family as of paramount importance. Modern woman is perhaps too realistic, and she can be heard to say of her loved ones: "Look at the creatures, aren't they awful? But they're my job!" So though she works like a Trojan for her family, her open eyes make her do it harshly, whereas blind devotion kept a certain bloom on life, even though a foolish bloom.

The exaggerated love of a mother can irk her family, but men can accept a degree of devotion from their wives that verges on deification. Seeing what devotion did to our fathers may be part cause of our present honesty, if honesty is not too good a word for the harsh exposure of every foible that many men receive from their wives. Though the new openness that now flourishes between men and women can be very good, it can also be a battle entailing great endurance in discussion. There is no denying that modern love is not restful, having much of moral warfare about it, yet it flowers with new life, and consider what other modes of love have been.

Women need to respect men, but how much do men need to respect women? Rather less apparently. Man needs to depend on woman blindly and he needs to delight in her; she is not respected so much as enjoyed and treasured. To a woman it is surprising that a man can respect himself if he does not respect the woman he loves, yet he accomplishes this frequently. When his wife's behavior is bad it is a private sorrow for him, but he is not dishonored as he would be if he failed in his work. While a woman, being a man's ally, cannot now respect herself if she furthers what she scorns. Her honor has always depended on the man nearest her, and it is a great change that today she wants it in her own keeping.

Man needs his pride, is in danger without it, and woman knowing this builds it for him without letting him see how much of it he owes to her; though also building thereby his vanity, the quality she dislikes most in him, and that she uses most often for her own ends. His

pride is the sign of his possibilities, and these are measured in the hierachy of his work, those above and below
him measure them, and he needs to be measured as it
matters profoundly who he is.

While a woman is contained in a small world which
she contains, where she gives herself without stint, more
a natural force than a person, and often careless as to
whether she is a tyrant or good incarnate. She may be
the least considered person in her world yet the most
needed; sometimes the one who gives life to the others,
and somtimes the one who holds them in life.

Modern women can be fiercely sensitive about pride
and about sacrifice, for they feel that giving is only giving if one is free to withhold. When it is assumed—for
these things are far deeper than thought—that sacrifice is
our natural role, that we even like it, and that as it is part
of our nature a little further sacrifice here and there is no
trouble to us at all, we are angered.

It may be our feeling for the very concept of love that
arouses us. For it seems to us that our best quality has too
often brought us low and brought love low; that we have
sometimes lived humility, selflessness, and charity and
that these have gained us many wounds. Too often we
have lived them in the unworthy forms of reflex agreement and unreal giving. So that now when we often refuse to give and seldom agree, our opposition rises from
wells that have been a long time filling.

Out of a desire to survive, and sometimes out of generosity, we have avoided all knowledge of our own view of
reality, and it must be this that we now seek. We hunger

for it, and we batter the man nearest us in order to find it, until many a husband leads a life of wild skirmishes and quick surrenders. He often gives up trying to reconcile his idea of what a woman should be with the surprising person who stirs up his home. His private life is the place where he is forced to abandon reason and take the full impact of experience. He can come to believe that a woman is nothing less than actuality, nothing other than what really happens—the life that at a given time two people were—so small wonder if he feels it fruitless to theorize about the living moment.

13

We No Longer Stay in Our Bodies

WOMEN are life-carrying vessels and the biological role affects the entire concept of women. Many women only reach their feeling through sexuality and thus know their greatest richness of experience. When a woman conceives it can release the deep layers of the unconscious and it may mean a moment of mystic participation when the body and spirit are one. Such a woman is transcended by sexuality, for it is the release of life that allows her a glimpse of transcendent truths.

The life of the body is so different for women that a man often has difficulty in understanding a woman's attitude. She serves life with her body, with her body she transforms and is transformed. It is through the body that she learns. Beyond the happiness of the body there is for her a discipline of impersonal truth which makes her forever astonished at man's just enjoying the body, or reviling it and needing to rise above it. She is both baffled and

[136]

shocked, and there is little doubt that the dissonance between man and woman lies in the body. A man may act as though the body existed for his personal pleasure or denial, but the life of the body initiates the woman into knowledge greater than her own, so she is bewildered that man has sometimes made evil out of her good, and has claimed to rise above what has been her door to understanding.

When a woman is with child the child claims her. She will be emptiness and she will carry her child as though she were a vase. Slowly she fills, sinking down into some deep river of women, submerged and almost lost. Then she rises triumphant and initiated, for a new person has been born from her body. She has been used by life and she is mute. Some of her has ceased to be and instead there is this ancient, helpless, closed bud of a stranger. She has given part of her being to him and he is her master. He is also her enemy for he will drive her to all her sins of excess. He is the one she will die to further. She does not know it yet, but as long as she lives her body and all her being will be under the compulsion of keeping him in life that the life in him may fructify. For even when she does it blindly and under protest, it is life she serves and often serves by not being.

She serves life in her child, she lives in him the miracle of his newness and of his having come into being through her. The relation between a mother and a child can be an absorbing love affair, for the child is guileless, trusting, and it sees no fault in the mother; so each is perfect for the other. Children accept good and evil as belonging together so that the failings of the mother do not count against her. The mother and child may be utterly united and the mother knows all promise in the child's promise; yet if she delights in him too much and too long, she can destroy what she created and then she is against life not for it.

It might be thought that a mother's first wish would be to help her child grow up, but much of her is against its growing up. She wants to prolong its indissoluble union with her. The child is safe then and so is her motherhood. Women may want to stay at this instinctive place because its close identity satisfies their primitive oneness. Some women find it easier to be mothers than wives, and if they have no knowledge of how to build a relation with their husbands, then this physical unity with the child holds them long. They want to keep each child a baby, spoiling him in an effort to keep him close as though only with a baby can they find contentment.

It is a temptation, for many women, to avoid relationship with the husband by using the child as a substitute love; which makes a conscious relation between husband and wife doubly necessary, as it is the only safe place to put adult love. The companionship and the sexuality that fail to find fruition with the right partner are almost bound to seep into a relation with a child of the opposite sex. That child is of course given more than he can take. He is given a richness of relationship that makes him find other children, and other young people pallid by comparison with the ensnaring parent. To have been so overfed emotionally in childhood is a great handicap, and it may render the grown child incapable of making a marriage of equality, perhaps being forced to mate with his own inadequacy.

When men achieve something by dint of hard work and ability they usually acquire some prestige and perhaps much wealth. A woman gives more intimately and completely than a man, and when her work is done she may have very little. She may only be rich by what she has given up. As she gave her body to house her child she felt that he belonged to her, belonged to her as nothing else could since he was made in her body, yet in no time at all her baby tried to belong to himself. How natural if she is outraged and bereft, and no wonder if she tries by indulgence and by bullying to prove to him that he is wholly hers.

She has to lose her battle and her child has to win, but he may win only a little of himself. She may keep so much of him that all his life he is hobbled, moves lamely and never lives his life freely or fully. Years later when she knows that her grown children are still hers, unable to belong to themselves, she has to suffer her sin; and though her children can right it if they will, she is helpless. When it is too late for her to mend she sees that her unconscious blindness was against life.

Yet she is caught in contradiction as always, for she must live in the intense identity of mother and child, the necessary identity that fosters the child's life. Nothing less than this gives the child the value he must have, and insures him the care that his wearisome demands might deny him. So a woman has to be utterly at one with her child and then by some insight, some high courage in letting him go, believe that her child belongs to himself. Here her paradox is at its most poignant, the paradox of giving and of giving up. Nothing less than love and wisdom are any use. She has to help the child to take possession of himself and help him to differ from her. Her love has to be sufficiently strong to give the child courage to trust himself. Her steadfast and open mind must show the child that conflict and difficulty are rightly parts of life, and seldom a cause for withdrawal.

Now how good all this sounds and what peril lies in every word. If a mother knows the truth of it in her heart and lives it sensibly and humanly, nothing could be better. If her head catches it as an idea she may interpret it as a direction to let the child do anything and everything while she applauds. She may conclude that toughness is the new good, and that she must delight in that. It could easily seem that her child is so little her own that she will have no heart to love him. Wounded in her natural tenderness, wounded that being a loving mother has become so complicated, she may become tough herself.

Any woman could say on reading this: "What is the use of advice? You know that children behave like angels and savages, that we're tired much of the time, and we're angry when we're tired. We do the best we can, and no matter what we do our children turn out to be quite ordinary." Yes, that is true. Nothing is as chastening as being a mother, do what we will we produce faulty human beings, but some of their faults are due to us.

When a man builds a bridge, there it is: a bridge. When

a woman bears a child, she brings forth an unknown possibility. Someone who may be an exception, who may be happy and perhaps creative. The child will live in the unknown future and the parents will try to prepare it well, giving it what they lacked, meaning to make none of the mistakes that were made with them. In their hearts they plan that their child will rise above them, and they sometimes dare hope that it will make the world a happier place. So a child is never just a child, but it is to some degree a new solution to the mystery of life, while a man never expected his bridge to be anything but a bridge. So how can a man and a woman feel the same about their life's work?

His bridge was only meant to be a bridge and as it was one, he was a good builder of bridges, while she after all her efforts was both a bad and a good mother. She made different mistakes from those her parents made but she made mistakes. Try as one will it is impossible not to be a bad mother much of the time. If your child has your own worst qualities you think they belong to the child and fail to cure them in yourself, which was your best hope. If your child differs from you greatly you may find its qualities alien and troubling and have no understanding of the child's needs. So we cause our children much suffering. We are their first experience of the hardness of life, and they learn their lesson young. This is not the way we usually look at ourselves, but it would be a gain if we saw this aspect of our great importance to others.

It is now understood that the child is contained for years in the psychology of the parents, sensitive to every conflict between them, with many of the problems in the child resulting from the problems in the parents. Motherhood is now seen to depend not on what we do to the child but on what we are in ourselves. Like all human relations it baffles rules, yet it seems safe to say that the best way for us to help our children is for us to learn to improve ourselves.

Modern mothers have heard so much of the harm they can do their children that it has created a despair among them. They openly declare their bankruptcy and very often they declare it to their children. Older mothers affirmed that they always knew what was best for their children, but now mothers depend on experts and have little faith in themselves. Experts have said that children must be free, as even their worst unruliness may be an effort to find their own independence, so now too many parents abandon all discipline and become the victims of their children. The parent has become afraid of the child.

Psychologists have rightly said that the overtrained child lacked individuality and that freedom built character. But this has been most calamitously misunderstood, for psychologists have said again and again that children must be contained and taught the boundaries of reality; taught what was safe and sensible to do and what was not, what was permissible and what was not. The child's freedom and experiments must be contained within a firm boundary, and this boundary is for the parents to create and maintain. It is hard to do and often it is not done.

From very conscientiousness mothers tend to relinquish

their role to the experts, almost asking society to take on their responsibilities. To be a mother is difficult and dangerous, but no one else can replace her. Will women never see how important they are? Their power of doing good and of doing harm is beyond measure, and it is done in private where no one can stop them but themselves.

Reports have been issued recently both in Great Britain and in the United States giving proof that mothers with children must stay in their homes. Dr. John Bowlby in the report published in Geneva in 1952 on *Maternal Care and Mental Health* states that the relation between the child and the mother is the steady center on which the child's later development is based. This report is the result of years of research showing that only a close, living relation teaches the child loyalty to one person, thus giving it a sense of value in itself and in another, and assuring it that a shared standard is worth serving even at the cost of suffering. Without this basis of human trust built up between the mother and the child, the child has no feeling that can be appealed to. It is also incapable of abstract thought, as only immediate gain satisfies its unappeased need, and no long-term meaning will be given heed.

These findings may well give women a renewed sense of the greatness of their task, but also of its difficulties. For though it is now proven that children need their mothers, which their mothers knew already, the situation has two sides, and a dual solution is called for. These reports make painful reading as they expatiate on delinquency and criminality resulting from a lack of maternal care; and most women will renew their efforts to understand their children, and to make their homes centers of sensible living. But with this as one point of balance there still remains the other. The fact that women want an interest outside their homes, that very often there is something they can do and want to do, and that too often financial need urges them to add to the family income.

The home is apparently no longer enough for women. Perhaps they do not always see what is needed of them there, which is often a quality of being, not doing. Many mothers are alone in the house all day when the children are at school, and they become restless with their own needs. It is the woman's masculine side that longs for creativity of a specialized kind, and this is a real need, but it often finds a bad outlet if it cannot find a good one.

It is true that the work in the home is both constant and dull. The woman creates order and cleanliness and presently they are gone. They were meant to be used and that is why she is needed to restore them, but the order and the disorder meet in the woman and they batter her into resentment. She wants to get out into the world where all seems more organized, perhaps measuring herself against modern industry and coveting its advantages. She wants to be saved by its efficiency, and she must be given every possible help, but it is also true that she must be expended at home, for her boundless giving is part of the natural good we still have.

The women whose ability has already established them in the outside world are often attempting the impossible task of doing two full-time jobs. When they have children and give themselves to a profession as well, their energy is drained by conflicting claims. But they persist in maintaining their exhausting effort, and that they do persist shows what a strain women are willing to endure in order to live both sides of their nature. Our sense says that a mother cannot do other work while she has young children, and our sense may be right. For though these women do both personal and impersonal things most capably, they do them at a great cost, and their children lose much. A woman whose mind and energy is absorbed in other things is not easily available for exchange of feeling with her children, so they often have no one to receive and know them. There is no one empty enough to let them give their growing selves. They may have every practical care, but they seem to have two preoccupied fathers and no perceptive mother.

The income contributed by the women who work makes it possible to have reliable care for the children, but it is relationship that the children need from their mothers and nothing else takes its place. So the contradiction is clear to see. It is vital for children and so for society that the mother reigns in the home, but it is apparently vital to many women that they spend much time out of it.

Modern education has trained woman for a wider life; she is wanted in the outside world and she functions well there. She is already living this dual life, there is nothing theoretical about it, it is in being, and if a woman cannot be educated without it making her extend her activities and her nature, is there not further and better support that can be given her? For the possibility of harm to the children is real.

The terms of employment for a woman with children could be different from those without children. A mother could be allowed three half-days a week, or she could work a six-hour day, or she might work alternate days with another woman similarly placed and trained. It seems a matter possible to arrange, and it is warranted both because a woman's quality is wanted in two places and because many women need to function in two ways. Though the utter contradiction between what life requires of women, and what they have come to require for themselves, could hardly be greater than it is.

Woman's willing heart has carried so much of the human burden, but she may well draw back from the task of seeing what she is doing. She could protest at being asked to look after everyone else and herself as well. Yet she has started down the masculine road and she can hardly deny that she is going two ways at once.

It is little wonder if she refuses to look at her present contradiction, since it is so baffling. It would tell her that if she remains unconscious she can do harm, and when she develops consciousness only to follow the masculine way she has but copied man's one-sidedness, and added her distortion to his. Yet—and here is our hope—if she finds a way to combine loyalty to the human value, while accepting the discipline of conscious understanding, there is a possibility of a new fruitfulness. One has to say again that so much has changed for woman that her own change was inevitable. The very fact that she now has few children releases energy that she has to meet and make safe for herself and for others.

Personal life is at a discount today. People work keenly, putting everything into their work, but many complain that their personal life is barren; so that one wonders why women who do not have to work have such a strong urge to do it. It almost seems that work has come to have a value that is unreal, and we take it as a drug, exciting and deadening. Women drive themselves when they are not driven by necessity, and everyone insists upon being exhausted. It is disturbing to see women so caught by activity, for the individual bond that used to matter most to women is a quality that is now doubly precious. The devotion we have all seen in woman makes one dare to say that as she tends to half relinquish her personal role, moving out into the impersonal world and allowing society to do what she was given by nature to do, that we are almost faced with being contained in the crowd as a substitute for being loved.

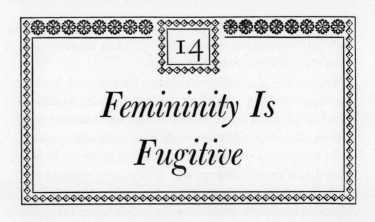

14

Femininity Is Fugitive

I t is the personality of the mother that creates the human temperature of the home, and what the mother is, is normality for the early years of the child. If she is a bonfire of a woman the temperature of the home is high but uncertain, stimulating but with irrational punishments. Strong emotions warm children yet also sometimes frighten them. Adult emotion can seem to them outside proportion and impossible to face; so an emotional mother can be the last person in whom a child can confide.

She cares too much, cares for the child's safety too much, and for justice, and right, and perhaps she cares too much for appearances. She may be so prejudiced in favor of virtue that she lacks the open mind confidences require. So her child may lie to survive, to keep life going and himself intact. If he does not lie after this manner he may have to distort himself into his mother's image of

him, destroying his own integrity to survive. So the
mother's temperament dictates the child's pattern. Is it
realizing all this that is more than modern mothers can
bear?

If a mother is a thinking type who lacks feeling, and
perhaps adds her own intellectuality to that of her husband, then together they may create a home devoid of
feeling. It may be a place of verbal gymnastics, of hardihood and lively stepping, but its lack of feeling can have
grave consequences. One of the children may have a
breakdown before the atmosphere in the home is noticed;
and even then the breakdown may still be attributed to a
weakness in the child, who was in reality carrying the
too heavy burden of the parents' incompleteness. So
women are fate to their children and nothing less. Our
children are fate to us, that too is true, for they show us
what we are, but we can seek understanding to help us
while our children are almost helpless against us.

Are we perhaps frightened by the extent of our responsibility? Has psychology itself brought this about by
attempting to make us understand our wide influence?
It is explained to us by experts, and to be read in every
magazine until women may feel that they will do less
damage in an office than they do in their homes. If
women are in flight from being women from very fear
of what they may do to others, then consciousness in
women is going to be a slow growth. Yet it seems unlikely
that we will find it any simpler to become masculine. Let
us take heart, for we have endured so much that understanding ourselves seems comfortable by comparison.

It takes courage to admit that our children are at our mercy, but we know it is true. We often feel that we are at their mercy, and we are, and we must preserve ourselves from them. They must be taught that they have no more right to consume us than we have to consume them, and it is better to do it consciously as a matter of decent behavior rather than as daily domestic warfare.

Our children are themselves from the moment they are born, tight packed beginnings of their future selves, but they are also fragile and indeterminate, and it is we who determine so much in them and for them. In childhood our girls can be masculine and our boys feminine. They are both bisexual to some degree and it is greatly in our hands to determine the balance. Small boys can be sensitive, hesitant, needing to be given courage, or they can be amoral, seeking the adventure of the effective act, wholly indifferent as to its consequences.

Little girls sometimes share this instinctive pitilessness with no feeling present to curb or soften them. Girls can on occasion be howling animals wanting to destroy, but they also tend to pause before suffering. They are made to succor helplessness and sometimes they remember that this is so. But again and again it is we who decide the balance, decide it and keep it right.

The masculine is so clearly present in some little girls and it is generally the mother who can still it, or who has aroused it. By the time a girl is two or three, aggressive behavior can burst forth that may be a just charge against the treatment the child has received. For if a little girl meets with irrational temper in her mother how else is she to defend herself? Her aggression and what amounts to a refusal to feel, is the child's refusal to have her feelings played on by adults. She faces arbitrary judgments and irrational anger with her own pitilessness, and so at an early age her parents have set the pattern of her behavior. It is they who have brought out her masculinity and made it her outward character, when it should have remained in her unconscious where it belonged.

Happily we also protect our daughters. The negative aspect of a girl's fate is accepted and ameliorated. She is wanted to be gentler than a boy, her voice softer, her ways kinder. We choose this for her and then it has to be made endurable. So appeasing women for being women begins early and too often it is unlimited indulgence. If the girl is pretty we enjoy admiring her and then to be enjoyed becomes her role. We must admit that for her good and for society's benefit we may create an emptiness in her life. And if we differentiate from the beginning between her hard and her soft side, has not much progress come from choices such as this?

Little girls do not like our prohibitions. They feel the excitement of the boy's rough play and they want to take part in it. It is we who protect our daughters from calling up the wildness that would come if we did not make the choice. They protest and feel curbed and confined. They can be as adventurous as a boy, though their adventures have a different quality from his.

From seven to twelve—let us say—a girl may be full of gusty action, her masculine side urging her to deeds of valor. She is a knight who rights wrongs, or a general who leads an army to free a beleaguered city. In her own eyes she may stand for romantic courage, and when she later relinquishes this side of life to the man she does it sadly, and often with some mistrust. Some of it has to be relinquished—how can it be otherwise?—yet the desire to retain some of it is another problem that makes us uneasy with ourselves.

When in an effort to prepare a girl for her feminine role she is told that later she will bear children, it seems to her a distant thing and stirs her little. At puberty she feels her chances of brave adventure slipping from her, and the guise in which she consents to go forward is uncertain— the kind of a woman her mother is being the strongest influence in her decision as to how much of a woman she has the heart to be.

This slow guidance is chief part of a mother's role, yet our innate quality probably has more effect than anything we consciously do. For our children we are measures of life, and at an early age they make their decisions as to whether we can be safely used.

Many men remember having chosen in childhood to be as their mothers were. If the father represented mas- culinity in too dictatorial a way, grossly domineering perhaps, then a sensitive boy may have preferred the fem- inine way. He has chosen to forego his strength and the struggle it entailed, and to range himself on the side of life that was pleasant and indulgent. He may have lacked the innate stamina and courage to summon his own force to oppose that of his father, but perhaps he preferred on moral grounds as well as on grounds of personal convenience to be gentle and long-suffering.

A child has a natural ideality. It is real itself, and looking at its parents from its own rightness, many a child is morally disappointed by his parents. If we remembered this in time our later years would know less regret.

Men who live from their feminine side often remember the scene, the unseemly quarrel, when they decided not to be like their father, and the mother too often proved glad of an ally in her fight with her husband. Thus she ensnares her son from his rightful masculinity.

Both boys and girls need great help in differentiating their secondary sexual characteristics. This has of course long been recognized and indeed considered so necessary that it has been done to excess. All that was feminine was thought to be bad for the boy, and all that was masculine was thought to be bad for the girl, until the great schools for girls became copies of the public schools for boys, and the distortion of women began in earnest.

Society has at different times and in different ways taken the severest measures to create men and women, particularly to create women—femininity being the desirable but fugitive thing it is—and now the whole matter seems again out of hand. But this may be because we are on the threshold of a much wider concept of both sexes.

The education of boys presents fewer problems than that of girls, but how is a girl to be kept within the natural circle that holds her, and yet given pride and pleasure in being there? How is the positive aspect of the prohibitions that surround her to be presented to her so that she will accept it as positive? Or must the negative aspect be accepted as right and good? There has to be great good assured her if she is not to have some resentment, or to insist on all the compensations of indulgence and overvaluation.

There must be better ways than those we know to prepare a woman for the duality that is inherent in her life, and an education to be a woman is easily imagined. But as no one agrees as to what a woman is or should be, she is educated as though she were a man, with the hope that if she marries quickly her education will not have done her much harm, and if she does not marry she will need all she got.

At one moment it seems nonsense to suggest that knowledge is different for women than it is for men, and at the next it seems even greater nonsense to think that what comes from the minds of men, and is interpreted and acclaimed by men can enter the mind of a woman as anything but a foreign body. If she is honest—if anyone is honest—it must seem a different thing to a woman than it does to a man, but do we leave reputable room for the expression of that difference?

A woman's role of adapting to others makes it so uncertain what may be required of her, and of what she may prove capable. She may inherit her father's brains and know how to use them. She may marry a statesman, or become a statesman herself, or she may have to maintain her family by taking in lodgers. She may not marry at all and then she may have to exist in her own right whether she likes it or not.

So in a vagueness about their own meaning that can amount to vacuity—girls grow up. Too often they lack definition and direction, they are frequently treated in a deprecatory manner that hurts their pride. Society receives from women what it has itself created, and women are only half to blame for what they often are.

Society might get a better return if it recognized the dignity of a girl's role, told her that her humanity is of paramount importance, asked her to have a great heart, warned her she would need incalculable stamina, said in forthright terms: "We grant you the right to be and do anything that is within your power, but we pray you not to mar your charity, or lose the way to your own heart."

15

They Dump Their Sins Down

How natural that society wants women to stay in their homes and make them happy places. A home has always been a refuge, and in this noisy crowd-age the individual craves a place where the individual values may flower. A place where freedom and quiet may still be found, where the unexpected and the idiosyncratic abound: where the individual is honored and where all happens because an individual liked, or believed, or loved. With all our hearts we want homes like this, we know that no one but a woman can make them, and of course we beg her to do just this.

Though homes are not always so good. Almost the same phrases can describe a place without freedom or privacy, a battleground where all behave badly and think it their right to do so, believing a home to be expressly provided so they may dump their sins down. One has to behave badly somewhere and where is it safe but in the home?

Who will stand colds and moods and tempers, and every possible reaction to the pressure of the world, but a wife and mother? This battering is inherent in life and must be received by someone, and the someone is the woman.

It is she who creates a home that will shelter unhappiness and happiness. It is she who works and makes possible the comfort and the quiet and the gaiety that others enjoy. Home is her workshop, often she is the one person who has no right to be ill in it, and usually she can only rest by getting out of it for a little. In a home where she does all the work everyone may feel guilty at what they receive, and take her temper as moderate price for what is given them. All this being true to some degree it is most natural that everyone begs women to remain in the home, for there they are needed beyond counting.

It must be mentioned that if a woman wants an interest of her own in her home her family may feel wronged, mock at her interest, and even say it is selfish of her to give it her attention. She may do the thing she likes to do rather badly, like the amateur she is. She may very well use her interest as a weapon to hit her family with, but she needs it as our lungs need air, and the delight of creative work to a woman who for years has lived for others, is an incomparable experience. She may have real talent, talent long neglected, or a new gift may appear in her middle years that she has never suspected was hers; but even if the gift is small it is a new creation, and let her treat it as her own true love, which it often is.

Today a woman is not only caught in the problem of her own psychology—which may be creative or destructive—but she is trapped by the sheer hard work in the servantless home. Very often she can not deal with herself until that time of blissful freedom arrives when her children are at school all day. Then at last she is less tired, and finally she meets herself. Up till then work and fatigue decide everything.

What can be done in a home is measured by the physical endurance of one woman. Her nerves and her temper go long before her muscles do. She and her husband often take on every job that requires to be done. They are as self-supporting as peasants or pioneers used to be. They have many gadgets to help them, and they have trained intelligence, but they no longer have the simple mind that accepts the necessity of the humdrum and the laborious. Necessity is no longer duty and destiny as it used to be. We are far too clever for such piety. We assume that we should be above necessity, that our good minds are meant to free us from dull duty.

When a husband and wife undertake most of the household repairs in order to save the expense of the expert, they are fully aware that they do not like doing it. They do the washing and cleaning and cooking, though they have machines to help them. They move the furniture, they do the painting and the carpentry, they mend the electric contraptions, and they do the garden; he goes on the roof to mend the chimney and down in the cellar to adjust the heating. In this list the children are not even included, for they come first. Very often it is one man and one woman doing these things in a house that was planned for servants. Many couples do all this, and they do it fairly cheerfully, but it irks them just because they are more educated and so more highly strung, and anxious to do other things; and so a part of them is in a state of protest, and that part gets in the way.

The man is often most reasonable about all the jobs he does. The woman protests rather more. She has just begun to get out of the home, but she is also in it deeper than ever. Her grandmothers may have rested all their dignity and calm on the responsibility and importance of their role, but many modern women are in rebellion against the demands a modern home makes. They do more menial work than their grandmothers did, and their minds are often more highly trained, so they are living two extremes of their nature.

Modern woman has her trained intelligence to help her and it does help her, but the strain she is under is there for everyone to see. Many of her personal tastes have been satisfied before marriage, and after marriage they often have to be given up. The minutia and monotony of housework bore her, while the impossibility of organizing anything into any given shape for any length of time makes her distraught.

A woman is seldom good at saving herself, and how can she be when she has always abandoned herself? She tends to give herself as completely to a cake, as to a lover or a child. Detachment is the most difficult thing in the world for her to acquire. She needs it to see herself and to save herself, but she gets very angry if this is pointed out to her. And the world must remember that it has asked attachment of her for a long time; what is more—it is still uncertain that anyone likes detachment in women.

So there are many aspects to a home, and one of them is in the mind of the woman who runs it. There is often a lonely, questioning mind that is carried around in a desperately busy body. The woman is the house. She is the concern and care and query felt about every item in every bureau drawer, and every bit of food on every shelf: wanting some food eaten, planning to get it into someone before it spoils, not wanting other food touched. With some plan or some despair linking her with every inch of the house, and with every quality of everyone in the house.

But in her mind there is often a cool question, followed by another cool question; one question treading on the heels of the next, the procession of questions going on and on, and never giving her any peace. "Is this marriage? Odd. Do I really know my husband at all? Well—not always. But does he know me? I wonder. How did I have these particular children? Strange. Are they what I expected? How could they be? Could I improve them? It doesn't seem so. Can I improve my husband? It would be unwise to try again. Anyway so soon. Can I improve myself? Oh heavens, what am I to do about myself?"

And so the questions go on and on in her lonely head. Is she responsible for what her children have become? Did she create, or fail to allay, the fears and weaknesses she sees in them? If she is responsible for their faults did she create their virtues? That is nonsense, for she would not have known how. But she has done harm. This is the knife in her heart. She can spoil, she can even ruin the thing she loves. So devotion isn't enough. If she wasn't so tired, if she had more time, but she is pulled by necessity, pulled here, pulled there. She needs four pairs of hands, eight ears. Her children, her husband, her house all need her and all misbehave if she is not theirs. The one thing she needs is a quiet center in herself from which to view them, deny them; where she can rest and replenish herself. She lacks it, and can she reasonably be expected to have a citadel of her own since she was never warned she would need it?

Sometimes she goes away to think it over. Away and alone, and calm and unhurried, and perfectly tidy and not tired, she is sure that when she gets back she can manage it all perfectly. She understands her family and she loves them, now she will manage everything. But once more at home, she is once more the stage on which the never-ending drama is played. The house and all its inmates are in her, beating on her heart and on her nerves and her body. Not the calm body she inhabited when on holiday but a tired drum that reverberates as life beats on it.

It is true that she creates the home, but she is not sure that she inhabits it. It seems to be inhabited by children and men whose ideas of comfort are seldom her ideas. She is apt to make an aesthetic arrangement of her home, it becomes her concept of beauty, or elegance, or respectability. She arranges it and would like it to remain as her plan of a desirable life. But her husband and her children want to use it, and so they bring it to naught.

They are constantly on the verge of destroying her picture, so that she has to let a masculine and youthful tide of life flow through her cherished pattern, granting the tidal wave full freedom, and thankful if the walls and ceiling retain the pattern she put upon them.

For a woman can contain her family, feel her heart full with their well being, and yet be strangely alone in her home. She may be obliged to have a tantrum just to show that she too has a right to behave badly in the home, and because she would like a nonexistent mother to comfort her.

There are even times when she feels a stranger in her home, for if you contain you are outside and you are alone, a part of you, that is. She gazes at her husband and says: "Now who is this man so lost in his thought?" For when he is deep in an absorbing idea he forgets those around him, there is no way of reaching him. His body sits there and that is almost all that can be said. It is chilling when a husband does not know what he eats, fails to see his children changing before his eyes, needing him and not having him.

She knows that men stand for impersonal ideas, she knows all about that, she agrees that we would all suffer a great loss if this were not true, but she can feel that impersonal ideas are inimical to her side of life. For her this is the great division between men and women and they can be enemies here. A crevasse gapes wide between them. In spite of woman's new fascination with the impersonal, and man's new concern for the personal, there is a natural opposition between the heart and head.

A woman can hate the impersonal, hate and resent it, though she may also long for it and revere it. Women are only beginning to relate to the impersonal, and when they imitate man's way, or steal his knowledge from him, or go into the impersonal to find him, they lose their own roots; but when the abstract separates the man and woman she becomes afraid of it and finds it inhuman. The individual can be forgotten in the significance of a general law, and a woman's very blood protests against this.

She has much right on her side, for when she sees a man caught by the fervor of thought, fascinated by the possibility of making life greater in the future, even using thought as a means of gazing into the future, she also sees that he makes daily life poorer by his neglect of it. He is thinking of something that he cannot communicate to her, that perhaps she could not understand: she is excluded, and his absorption can seem so unrelated to life that for her it has something of madness in it.

She does not know where her husband is in time or space, and all she knows is that the reality of the day is denied. Birds at the window, sunlight on the wall are unseen, the man has no time for them, and she feels that time is passing. She wonders if she exists beside this driven man, if this is living; and she is sure a wrong is being done. Often she is right, though the immediacy of her point of view can be the very density of limitation for him. Even when his care for the impersonal is right for him and her care of the personal is right for her, the two rights can make a wrong, and the man and the woman feel far apart.

When a young married woman with children is seen wholly in her home, with nothing outside but her lonely mind groping for understanding, one might say: "But at least she is wholly feminine, nothing masculine there surely, except of course her troublesome thoughts."

Such a surmise shows that we are much simpler than life ever is. A young married woman may be greatly bedeviled by her masculinity though she can exhibit her blindness to it in her own special way. She may even summon up her masculinity to prove her love. Anxious to partner the intellectuality of her husband she becomes intellectual in season and out of season. If he has theories —a scientific mind—she can make love with pedantry. Her pride in his ability makes her march behind him like an army with banners, and too many trumpets. Giving herself as a woman does not seem enough to her, so she gives herself as a man as well, in order to have nothing left.

Homes do strange things to women and one of the things they do is to leave her empty. She can give thirty years of her life to maintaining a home, caring for the house and those in the house, living for others, and at the end they have all gone into their lives, and she is left empty. She has nothing and is nothing. The change from the years with too much to do to the years with nothing to do is so great that she may—sometimes, oftener than is known—come to resent her selflessness. She may have to drink the sour dregs of devotion, and sometimes, after a lifetime of giving, she attempts a belated selfishness. Such women try to find a self they have never had, attempting selfish ways that are wholly foreign to them, convinced that when they are crabbed and thrawn they are at last claiming their rights.

No one could have a heart hard enough to say they should have begun earlier and begun differently. And after seeing their unhappiness dare we believe in selflessness as wholly good? Many may have lived by its goodness, many may have received only good from it, but when they see its end then—if you are a woman—you want to dedicate giving in order to make it safe. To make it a gift to life, not just to certain people, so that it rises from a deep spring and the giver is nourished by it to the end. But perhaps unthinking giving is natural to us, and resentment at the end is natural too. For both are wholly human.

It may all be due to woman's primitive identification with the things she loves. For women are primitive. It is primitive to be both passive and receptive, all or none in your reactions, lacking all detachment, so we give constant proof that we are primitive. Well—it is painful to even glance at such an idea, while to accept it is both humiliating and infuriating. Our blind loyalty has been our greatest effort, and has seemed our greatest good. Then where are we since detachment and devotion are equally uncomfortable, and equally criticized?

This is where we are, at the point where we see these

two things in ourselves, and seek to balance them. We are undergoing a most painful change, a change that feels like a birth where we are doubly participants in the birth pains, giving birth and being born.

16

A Promise of Living Riches

WOMAN's present thirst for the impersonal is so strong that one could almost say she has fallen out of love with man, and fallen in love with the impersonal. Her independence and accomplishment declare this allegience, the demands made on her lead her further along the road, and she delights in the way she is going. One has to agree that she often finds the man within her own nature more exhilarating than other men, and that she would in brief rather be interested than loved.

Of course the fascinating fellow within woman's psychology has always been an integral part of her nature, of this we have become aware, but why is she living him so markedly now? Has she summoned him up to make some great change, or because she is driven so hard by events that she cannot do otherwise?

What is striking is that so many women are turned toward the impersonal long before marriage. They are stirred by learning, by some aspects of the arts, music, science, or affairs, before they are stirred by love. They have early formed an allegience to something that they may not be able to take into marriage, which may indeed leave a great deal of them outside marriage.

The wife's affair with the impersonal before marriage has a very curious resemblance to the ritual marriage that in much earlier societies used to take place in the temples. This may have prevented the full impact of marriage being too great, and perhaps the first night being offered to the god allowed the bride and bridegroom to meet in their simple humanity. That first pledge to the impersonal may have made marriage easier, but if present-day women are wedded to the impersonal without knowing it, it may make marriage more difficult for them.

Many women have learned to live successfully in a communal situation where everything is highly organized and where the issues are large. When they marry they enter a small, isolated, and very personal situation, and they are at a loss. Their collective side has become very capable and it is upsetting for a woman to find that she is not at all good in a personal situation. Her husband notices it, too.

He may seem to her rather small and very personal, just one human being in fact, which of course is what he is. He now takes the place in her life where before marriage there was a large organization. This is hard for both of them. The old roles of husband and wife no longer fit the situation. He does not now represent the outside world to her since she knows it almost as well as he does. Nor

can he be said to introduce his wife to the masculine
world, for she has been living that in her own right.

Here of course, is the new element, as women now live
their masculinity in their own right and like doing it, the
man no longer has the importance of doing it for them.
He is thus reduced in the eyes of his wife, and so in his
own eyes as well. She has become collective and wants
him to be as big as society, which he can't be, while he
hopes to find the personal in her and she hasn't got it.

Nothing is more striking in our modern scene than the
quiet and harmonious men, contrasted with the discordant
and noisy women. The men could often be called retiring,
but it would hardly be said of the women. Their direction
is markedly outward, while those men whose fate it is to
live the new value that rises from the breakdown of the
old, tend to be turned inward. One has to suppose that
this has happened because man in general has gone too
far in his development of the rational, and has thus
created a world too barren to nourish him. So now many
men are soft-mannered, reserved, sometimes guarding a
concern with new creative values.

Poets and writers speak from these places saying things
that puzzle and irritate, but which proclaim the missing
thing. They are saying that the world needs feminine oneness from which to be reborn, that humanity now having
seen its power to destroy, thirsts for love and mercy and
that the way to new life lies through the individual soul.

If many men have gone to their sources for very life's
sake, and many women are out in the world for sur-
vival's sake, what happens when they meet? Well—some-

times, one knows, there is mutual dismay and mutual wounds received and given. The man needs, as he has always needed, the woman to symbolize his feeling; with feeling lived and honored he is rooted, and so free to exercise his strength in the outside world.

Instead she lives the gallant experienced man she has learned to be. Depth of receptivity is absent. The feminine oneness with life may be more in the man than in the woman. The husband would have to be a hero indeed to rescue the wife from the tyranny of her inner man, and husbands have so little time to be heroic. So the man is baffled and weakened because he offers the woman feeling that only half dares flower, and she looks askance at it, having no idea how to nourish it. Each turns toward the other the unwanted side and their is confusion and pain.

One might take a dark view of it all. A man could say that a woman must guard personal values, that only in her can he find them; that only the mother can give the children the security that allows their feeling-life to grow; that only thus are individuals nourished. He could add that the quality of humanity matters more than anything else, any other achievement seeming easier than the training of a noble nature. If all this is said we can only give full and heartfelt response.

But a woman might say: "This thing has happened to us and must be lived through. We are caught by a side of our nature that we need and have too long lacked. We pay for it with bitter conflict and we know our husbands pay, and our children though they gain as well, and society gains hands down. So give us time. We can not do the heavy tasks that are required of us without the man in our nature. Don't blame us, for we carry a double burden, and we are trying to endure duality and to understand." To that also one would give most heartfelt assent.

So what does it all mean? Is there a new balance forming between the masculine and the feminine both within men and women, and between them? If this is so may it not be a new promise, a new hope? A new integration hardly begun and only barely glimpsed. It will entail more new things though many of them are already among us. It will certainly mean a new standard of relationship where we must attempt to relate to our partner uniquely, in a way not possible for any other two people; accepting that men and women need each other to become themselves and are only partly themselves if alone.

Think what has happened hitherto. We imagine that we fall in love haphazardly, but it is seldom so. Marriage would not be the mortal combat it sometimes is if our choice was not less simple, and more meaningful. When one looks into the psychology of two people united by love or hate—or a mixture of the two—falling in love seems to be a uniting with that part of ourselves of which we are least aware.

Nature confronts us with what is truly ours, and in the blindness she puts upon us we accept our worst and our greatest possibilities. We take on the hidden sides without which we are not ourselves. It does not seem like this to any two lovers, certainly not at first. At first and for some time both are "in love"—with "a few difficulties," but "not bad really." Then after some time each begins to see his own fault in the other and of course dislikes it intensely, finding it alien and wholly unacceptable, the one thing he cannot abide. Then the combat begins. Each hammers at the other, clamors that the matter must be put right. Now the fault is seen so clearly that hardly anything else is visible, the weak evasion, or the arrogance, or the hardness is seen and hated.

We are truly driven to dealing with it, but in the other, not in ourselves, since we are sure it is wholly theirs but not ours. We have strong opinions about it now, but how often do we ask ourselves: "I chose to marry someone as hard as this, why? Am I hard? Or am I so soft and cowardly that I have asked someone else to live my hardness for me? It must have great meaning for me since I am confronted with it daily, in the one I love the most and hate most often. Is this the unique conflict at the very core of my being, is this truly me?"

If by courage, insight, and grace of heart—or by just the wear and tear of marriage—we gain the humility to see that this quality in our partner is also in us, that it is mutual, indeed unites us, is the very dark spot in us that most needs our redeeming acceptance, then we may reach a wholeness that was perhaps the fullness and goodness foreshadowed in the first enhancement of love.

By living our latent sides as so many of us are now doing —or more often being lived by them—are we too stupid thus to learn that they exist, are within us, and are tearing us to pieces? And that if we but possessed the wit to see it, these sides comprise the wholeness that awaits us if we would make it ours. But if neglected, are the evil which belongs to no one, yet exists and shames us. There is such promise of living riches here that very caution makes us pause, remembering how all through time men and women have wronged each other.

If we only say—and surely we can go this short distance —that our present plight is a chance of self-knowledge that might prevent our planting on our partner our own worst fault. Even this might bring a new peace between us, and if a man learns to honor his feeling, and a woman becomes responsible for her masculine thought and will, there might be a new clarity between man and woman, and perhaps a new ease in giving the love each longs to receive.

Relationship

THERE have been times when women felt that relationship was little more than a wish to which they clung, but this is no longer true. They now have grounds for believing that it may be part of a new value, an idea widely served if also travestied. Two people united but at variance are no longer willing to just endure one another. They want to know why living together can be almost unendurable. If it can on occasion—indeed on many occasions—be more painful than living alone, why then is it felt to be more realistic, more alive, and much more desirable to be married than single?

One has to be realistic about solitude itself in order to answer this. For living alone can seem a state of self-respecting, heroic order compared to the hot turmoil of relationship. To live on good terms with oneself one has to have many of the major virtues, while marriage covers every known fault and yet is thought well of, sought after, and envied.

It does of course place you solidly in society, you are in a house—sometimes—and you can be seen carrying your human responsibilities. After marriage it becomes more clear who you are, since you have taken on a given role. You have ended that uncertainty of the unmarried, you have taken roots and there is reason to hope that you will now become a solid citizen.

Our age is so gregarious that there is at present a marked prejudice against anyone being alone. It is looked down on, and a need to be alone is almost considered a fault, a weakness, as though if one cannot endure—more—enjoy being with other people every minute one is aloof, unreal, and somehow to be pitied. But aloneness is not our subject, and there is no need of praising it, of stressing its rare felicities and deep insights, for one need only remember that creative ideas come to the individual when alone, and that most works of art are developed in the sharp awareness of solitude.

But we have been looking at marriage from the outside. From the outside it is reassuring to know that so much drama has been safely boxed into a home where it is hidden and taken care of—to some extent—by the inmates of those homes. But what about the people who are shut up in those homes, who are in fact those incredible dramas themselves? What is their great gain in marriage, so great that though they are constantly occupied with the intolerable faults of their mate—only the worst moments of marriage are referred to—they would be inconsolable if they had neither mate nor home?

Comfort as a reason for liking marriage is put aside, for think of the discomfort; having found a place to put oneself—and this is an immense gain—has to be discarded as chief solace, for so often the place seems a mad roundabout from which one would jump if one dared. There must be something other that makes marriage desirable, and makes it even at the bad moments better than being alone.

Could it be quite simply that one is known? That by living with an entirely different person, and finding them at times almost oneself, as well as utterly different, you each become actual to yourself? You know yourself more and more acutely, know yourself without possibility of denial. You live your life and no matter what happens, life has become actual to you. One hardly dares to say that love is the core of the relationship, though love is sought for and created in relationship; love is rather the marvel when it is there, but it is not always there, and to know another and to be known by another—that is everything. It sometimes seems the one thing to be avoided, but that is the mere frivolity of panic, which can deliver us over to the greatest loss of all—never to have become oneself and never to have lived one's life.

The intense awareness of the solitary person is so precious that for a lover of solitude to be much with others is like mixing with flotsam in a choppy sea; an experience of being endlessly jostled without hope of harborage. But tiring as too much companionship is, one can have solitary hours even when married, though it may require stratagem to secure them. Even if married we will contrive to hide ourselves. Poor shivering egos, what else are we after much of the time? We evade each other, we evade all knowledge of ourselves, we pretend and we lie, we do everything to avoid the naked humility of relationship. But marriage does force it on us in spite of all our efforts to avoid it, and gradually we are known. It is being known that makes marriage into relationship, that makes us capitulate and admit we are ourselves, and when a companionship has lasted a long time we each become a witness for the other; a witness of all we have been, until each is vested and proven in the other.

Strong people can be solitaries though they may pay a heavy price for its great good, but ordinary people need to live with each other. We grow dim if no one knows us, dim in our own eyes, and often very dim indeed in the eyes of society. We can grow into strange shapes if too much alone, if we never have the solace of real intimacy we may even break under the burden of our isolation. While fully known we are then caught by life, we cannot escape and we are thankful that this is so.

Once known we can no longer believe in our tight little ideas about ourselves, or about the other person, or about men and women, or about right and wrong. We are knocked out of our prejudices and preconceptions. We are exposed, dreadfully and meltingly exposed. Oughts fall down like ninepins, musts become foolish things, truth hardly needs uttering, for it is there, felt, and seen, and known to both.

Knowing and being known makes it clear beyond all need of argument that the incurable in each is always present, and must be carried as part of the whole; and in spite of this it is delicious to be together. And in spite of this delight both men and women enjoy the absence of the other, finding it also delicious to cease all compromise and adapt to no one. It becomes equally clear that men and women hate each other as well as love each other, and that it is natural to both to exploit, confuse, and even to betray each other. That each tries to dominate, feels safer if he can, and that recrimination is often only a sad attempt to survive; that when the man thinks the woman inferior, and the woman thinks the man a vain child to be hoodwinked and spoiled, both have turned down a cul-de-sac from which they must return. It is of course clear that there is a part of both that is outside marriage— the painful truth being and hurting more when un-admitted—that this is sometimes good. For if we were wholly contained in marriage we might be stifled as well as contained.

Knowing all this we still have to learn that the need of union is partly the longing to be carried, the clamor to hide in the other, and that the dark side of love is a desire to be relieved of the burden of being oneself. And we must learn as well, until we are forever convinced of our own nothingness, that we half want the other to be small. Our shame is that both men and women fear anyone bigger than they are themselves, and even try to reduce the other that they may not be themselves overwhelmed. We can each be so small and full of fear that we rail at the nascent life in the other, in very terror that we may have to pay homage to something different and greater than we have known before.

All of this, all of this is part of being known. Only a small part is true of each of us, but that part may show nakedly and unmistakably when we are together. Yet if seen—seen and admitted and forgiven—we can then come very near to being shriven. So that relationship—and one says this great thing with much hesitancy, but also with conviction—comes very near to following the injunction "Be ye priests one to another." So that at those times when honesty, mercy, and charity are in charge something may happen that is nothing less than safe inclusion of evil.

This aim and effort is difficult, diabolically, daily difficult; but it has the priceless advantage that it restores to love something that is almost leaving it, in our easygoing sandaled similarity. It restores danger to love, where it rightly belongs. The danger that one sees in some Spanish dances where the man and the woman move gravely in ritual steps because they are reality to each other. For with our passion for making everything easy, foolproof, understood, all danger and difficulty bypassed and only the easiest enjoyment wholly modern, we have increasingly denied—until we assumed it was true—the tension and the danger that lie between man and woman.

Since they attract, complete, and repel each other they rightly fear each other. One would be a great fool if one was not afraid of having one's reasoned judgment taken in charge by the instincts, of becoming blind to glaring faults that everyone else sees clearly, and that one saw clearly oneself a month ago, even a moment ago. It ought to be terrifying to lose our hold on our own identity, and of course it is and ever will be, no matter what nonsense of the moment we pretend. Love is such a high adventure that it is understandable—if pitiful—when we marry someone who hardly affects us at all in order to keep a firm hold on our own small ego.

So relationship shows as a large affair including practically everything, inclusion of course being its very essence. It is an all-out wrestling match with the humdrummery of life, it is at rare moments the play of the gods, and over and over it is the stripping of merit from each and the need of mercy. It is also delight, but the good things are too good to be touched on, and it is seldom wise to examine them.

Already too much has been said, so that now a reader may think that he—or she—has the hang of relationship, sees how it is done, and feels practically certain of making no further mistakes. In fact, has become an adept at living by reading a few hesitant words. Having noted that honesty was praised, this poor reader is now prepared to be honest to the bitter end, confident that honesty will work, and is altogether so misled as to have no inkling that honesty is barely possible between any two people; and particularly between any man and any woman whose sensitive selves are exposed to each other. For we must treat honesty as we would a bomb set to explode the next minute; only prevented from going off by our pity, only made safe to carry and display—and that only barely—by the knowledge that if we are too honest we may destroy what we build with tender care.

Perhaps one of the reasons—indeed the central reason —why relationship is difficult for men, even irritating to men, but natural to women, is that it is inherently contradictory. It flourishes best when conducted near that province where many women feel so completely at home, on the knife edge of the paradox. A man can say, and he may feel sure and strong in saying it, that a thing is one thing and not another. For many men no one thing can be both itself and its opposite. He is right or he is wrong, he is loved or he is not loved. It cannot be both ways at once. This is when he errs from clarity; but this clear and concise way of thinking is his specialty, and we should have got nowhere without it. But to many a woman it is not even sense, it is arrant nonsense and gets things into a pretty muddle. Indeed has got woman herself into a pretty muddle, and almost convinced her many a time to her own undoing, and man's as well.

What she clearly sees and knows by her own process of knowing—one not easily described but presently to be attempted—is that everything that matters is both so and not so. Men choose a viewpoint and build an impressive edifice on it, an edifice that may be impossible for the woman to wholly comprehend; but by choosing his materials he has, for her, broken the wholeness of things, and all the bricks he has left lying are, for her, the errors in his thought. She watches his edifice grow, she realizes the skill in its building has been great, but her very presence is its contradiction.

For her things are both so and not so, she loves, dislikes, yet still loves. That is the link she makes in life. The link between incompatible things, and between conflicting facts; and when a man makes the same link, as he constantly and blessedly does, he is living in her way and in his own feminine way. She would like love to encompass utter disagreement, since to her love only begins to seem truly love when it can. She can sometimes love and not want, love and not hate though a hateful thing is present, and she sees it as hateful. For let us ask once more, what else has she been asked to do with her love through all time but to include the hateful, and to live contradiction?

Man's simplicity about woman's way of life makes her limp at his side, and she marvels when he expects her to agree with him because she loves him. Her agreeing is his favorite proof of love, so—she has agreed. And only see what it has done to them. Women know that so much agreement puts women themselves outside morality. They also know how often much of marriage lies outside morality. Women have agreed until they have borne children to men they did not even respect. So how can women respect themselves? They have forwarded many a thing they would have stopped if they had not had to agree. When will man be strong enough to accept decent disagreement from his wife as from a friend? Though agreeing instantly and strongly—what a pity one cannot write down two things at once—that agreement is the essential diplomacy of life and forever necessary; that it is charity, but enforced it is ignominy for both.

One knows—with a sinking heart—what man does face from woman, and what a flight of unreason her disagreement can be; but that is the terrible vagary that is her shame, and has often been her sole safety. It is also the wild leap of the masculine fellow that woman is only beginning to realize is her reason and her unreasonableness, and who clamors to be taken in charge. Surely by now, men will admit that it is dull to be agreed with, and also dangerous. For the moment comes for every man when he needs honesty opposite him, offering reality to look into, mirroring truth clearly; and because he has asked for agreement too often nobody is there, only an echo comes.

Yet when man denies woman, he is probably asking her to let him have his undivided mind and follow his own way without doubt because then he is one, not two. Is he not saying that if he listens to her he is then pulled in two ways and so weakened? He often needs to ignore the duality she represents. Consciousness of good and evil reached man through woman, it was she who gave him the terrible knowledge, and she still represents this conflict to him. The conflict that forever lies between hard and soft, thought and feeling, togetherness and separateness, the clear impersonal and the confusion of the personal. She may also represent the intolerable future task of containing and surmounting all these. He still tries to evade this painful duality by believing in clarity, while she still says: "There are two ways, not one."

It can look as though love has always been—as much as there is any sense in saying that love has been one thing when we all know it has been everything—but let us take a stand and say that love has been the need of man to define himself as against woman, and then to see in her the qualities that completed him. She has reflected him to himself, and if it so happened that she was someone in herself this could be an undesired complication, blurring his image of himself. So it is not surprising if woman now wants a way of love that is an exchange between two; but even so dauntless a person as a woman sees how difficult a thing this is going to be to bring about, and how many things are inherently different for man and woman. She does not see how there can be agreement about the body. Bodies agree, their agreement is the one simple good between man and woman. But men and women think about the body so differently that their minds turn it into constant cause of war between them. The poor body—not honored enough for its goodness—frequently lived so that it cannot be honored; and often treated as though we could deny our minds with our bodies; and sometimes treated as though we could reach the spirit without being born into our bodies.

If man is "woman's work," as he is said to be, then it is high time that both men and women look more deeply into women's activities. If his being her work means that she supports and tends him, indulges and reflects him, until she is alone with the truth she never voices, except when her tongue ejects poison, then the recklessness of man is past belief. His being "her work" can mean many regrettable things, but it can also mean that his soul is greatly in her keeping, his insight and his honesty and many of his possibilities are held in her hands, so that her "work" is not safe for either unless she has great qualities, and man would do well to know that he needs the best in woman.

When man must be thought superior because he is a man, then woman is crippled by the inferiority she sees in him. It breaks her spirit more than the knowledge of her own inferiority. Her being alone with her sad knowledge of man may be—must partly be—the predicament that forced her to find her strength and her mercy, so the gain is there. But if she has built her good out of his poverty, and he feels the stronger for thinking her weak, might they not enjoy the change of seeing the virtue of honesty in each other, and perhaps many other virtues as well?

It would be entirely possible to call our present day frankness honesty, the tiresome attack and counterattack that many couples carry on in public as a display of humor. A reducing of each to knockabout partner, both wanting apparently to make the other little more than pitiably grotesque. But the honesty that women now seek is something other than this, more private a thing and a kinder thing, more a mannerliness of the heart, sometimes amounting to openness of the heart and a willingness to let truth enter in.

If truth did enter the heart of many a woman it would encounter bewilderment there; woman's old bewilderment that the superior need the mercy of the inferior, and that the strong ask strength of the weak; while still needing to think poorly of the weak, and still claiming that man's weakness must be hidden from him, as well as woman's strength. It is this dishonesty in man's thought that is the cause of bitterness in woman, and it can need all her masculine discipline and valor to contain what she sometimes thinks of man.

When truth is present in a woman all this becomes clear, and the woman points out to truth that man's blindness makes a hole in the fabric of sense which she used to darn with patient stitches. But she now wants to say quite simply: "There is a hole." Or even: "This hole has become too big to mend." She may ask truth if she can decently go as far as saying that, and truth will probably answer that she could hardly do less. Then greatly heartened, she might go a step further and ask: "May I say to man: 'Could you carry a little more of your own weakness, because I find I must take on more of my own strength'?"

If truth nodded encouragement they would then wait for man's answer. It would be of the very greatest importance what answer came, since woman's carrying of man's weakness may have been the creative bond between man and woman; and if this is so she has to make sure that the new bond holds before she breaks the old.

Having invited truth into her heart his light plays everywhere, which is painful for her, indeed very painful because it is only half natural for her. She is not accustomed to awareness that is a bright light; she has usually learned by participation, by wanting the happiness of others more than her own; often not wanting a thing unless someone else found happiness in it. She has

learned by being empty for herself but full for others, she
has learned by being vague and by being kind.

When she contains others she knows many things,
though not herself of course, but she extends into many
people, she is rich, she is alive, she is almost boundless;
but on the new path she has taken she can put a fence
around herself, a fence of intellectual concepts that nothing can pass. Thinking can so isolate a woman from her
feeling that no matter what is said or done she cannot
receive it. She has lost the power to receive, and in the
degree to which this has happened she has ceased to be
a woman. When a woman is caught in this lonely trap,
nothing will free her but realizing that she must think and
not think; which is not easy to do, but is possible and
even natural to woman.

If she escapes the dangers of the head and her own
truth continues to shine in her heart, all may be well. If
she thus learns in what has always been her true way,
much becomes clear and she is ready to let it be seen by
others. She sees that her fundamental position of containing man, of waiting to receive life through him places
her in a position of fundamental helplessness. This is her
true helplessness and man respects it, but to let the idea
of her helplessness go into every aspect of life is great
nonsense, making nonsense of a thousand things. Because
she is at the center of man's life her power is terrible, and
it is as often he who is helpless before her, as she is before
him. She is as implacable as she is helpless, and very often
as intelligent. Both men and women know that this desperate contradiction is true, so the helplessness of woman

is a game played between man and woman, and perhaps the strength of man is another game.

Having invited truth in for her purpose he now loiters for his own. He shows her that her constant preoccupation with man will never let her know more of man than what he is with woman, with one woman, with herself in fact. That a man needs to be without a woman to be truly man, that he is child not man if he cannot be without her; while she is more a woman when with him. With him she has a chance to live her best side, while with her he may live his worst. To meet her he may capitulate too much, living his poorest femininity until her demands can disorientate him wholly.

It is always dangerous to look into one's own heart and she sees her idea of herself undergoing so radical a change that she becomes conscious of great disillusionment. Then she knows that her heart is full of disillusionment, with the world's impasse, with the world as man has made it, and she knows that she is disillusioned with man. She is appalled at the threat to life that hangs over us, and doubly appalled because she sees that man, too, is helpless. This is very frightening to her, but she takes it as a summons to give, and also as a summons to examine who she is, for that would determine the quality of her gift.

18

Love

WHEN a woman loves and when she is loved then there are periods, even long periods, when no problem exists. Love makes her role good, sometimes hallowed, while a lack of love received or given can make her role intolerable. Accepting the will of her father in place of her own was once loving protection or galling frustration, according to the love felt by both. Submitting her body to her husband is still either outrage or consummation according to the love in each. Carrying the child she has conceived is good or bad in precise measure of the love or hate that impregnated her. The birth of the child, its suckling and rearing need her love and the love of others for her.

She needs love through all these things, for they mark her great dependence; the dependence created by nature and much of which she will never escape. Perhaps she should not escape it, for if she did not need help through all these periods there would be less goodness in the world.

Later on she needs love to let her child go, and later still when the child is grown she needs great love that no one can help her find, but which she has to create in her own heart, in order to let her adult child have his right to sin and fail and suffer and die. If there has been enough love she will be able to give to her children the final gift of relieving them of her need of them. So love seems to be the basic truth for a woman, the chief thing in her life, and the one thing to which she must never be untrue.

But this is not saying little, it is saying everything. No one would say love is simple, or easy, it is barely understandable and sometimes barely endurable and it includes everything. Everything asks to hide under the cloak of love, no height and no depth is outside its empire; it is asked to eke out every lack and to work every miracle. There is no richness and no ardor and no disillusionment it may not be asked to encompass. It is frequently expected to sin and it is often regarded as sin. It is acknowledged as the greatest good and everyone pays lip service to it, yet how quick all are to revile it, to kill it, and who can be counted on to recognize it and respect it?

It is sometimes the enemy of the spirit, though the spirit is more apt to be the aggressor against love than love against the spirit. Love and spirit are ill at ease together, and this is one of the tragic discords in life for life needs them both, and it hardly needs saying that life needs the body. But the spirit has no tenderness for the body, even fears the body, and at times the spirit seems

afraid to face love. It is true that love is often not fit to face
the spirit, so there is war between them. This means war
between man and woman, for the desires of a man's body
are often stronger than he is, while at other times he
punishes his body, apparently would be better pleased if
he lacked a body, and distorts his humanity in his effort
to transcend his body. While the woman troubled and
puzzled can only say: "I give bodies and I give them with
love."

So this division between man and woman remains, and
if woman's way is to heal division she is often baffled here.
It can seem that woman has yet to find her own spirituality. She possessed it once, and there were goddesses of
life and wisdom, of intelligence and of healing, and of
destiny. But the patriarchal religions have brought us a
long way from that, and have perhaps separated woman
from herself so drastically that her own spirituality lies in
the future, and she has yet to find her way to it.

The longing for love that both men and women feel,
the clamor and grasping for love obviously does not come
from full hearts that must give; full hearts usually over-
flow quite simply and with little fuss. The great to-do
about love is more like the starveling bay set up by hunger. Our emptiness must be filled, our nothingness must be
denied. We thirst for love's denial that we are small, we
want its reversal of truth, its enhancement of value, its
turning of aloneness into uniqueness. We rave to be given
ourselves.

The want of love can be near to the dark night of the
soul described by mystics, giving all life a sandy dryness,

an emptiness as though one heard hollowness and heard it in oneself. This terrible want is in many people, for it is common to go without love; and men and women, the married and the unmarried, can feel that they have missed the central experience of life because they have known little love.

Yet some do—almost by dwelling on what they have not had—come to know love so well that they can be said to be "in" love. Such love is not directed toward any particular person, it does not seem to need that, it is more as though one at last reached the quiet of a place that arrives in us, and the need of love lets us go. But this may only happen late in life, and the problem of love is not only a problem that lies between men and women, but it is the problem of the soul in both men and women. It is almost the measure of the quality of the individual soul. Because men often leave their love to be looked after by woman, counting on her to keep it alive, in good heart, and worthy of trust when needed, it becomes a very serious matter if there is any danger of woman forgetting love's great importance.

That love will exist as sexuality, as vanity, and as social diversion one takes for granted, and it is nonsense to deplore this or that manifestation, since each kind of person loves in his own way. What he is his love is. But for a woman love is a much greater thing than for a man, as it is almost her reason for being; it is the place where her quality is of supreme importance, since the quality of love she represents may be the best of life those about her will ever know.

Now when so many women live lives more collective than personal, and function from their heads rather than from their hearts, how are they to keep near those sources of feeling which rose naturally in simpler times? Women now almost have to make a conscious effort to preserve their own humanity, and this includes learning how to remain "in" love as though it were a state of consciousness rather than a tie to a single person.

Let it be said quickly that affability is not referred to, or any bright graciousness of behavior. We already do that very smoothly indeed, we are almost as good at it as though we were machines. It is a much more serious affair altogether of which I speak. Our masculine side has become so strong and leads us so far afield that we are now forced to make a conscious effort to keep in touch with our own femininity, remembering that it is our first loyalty.

If it were not too fantastic to say—but surely we can risk some fantasy in such a cause—I would say that we must regard our inner balance as so vital that we must wish, and will, our masculinity to impregnate us with understanding. If we receive insight as though it were life itself, and then endure the long gestation of its teaching we will surely bear the child Humility. When we find it is we who need compassion we will also have it for others, and we may become loving enough to sometimes forego liking. With our feeling alive and sentient we are safe, or fairly safe.

All this may sound impossibly subtle, but it is not subtle, it is suffering, the ordinary suffering of living and growing, and it is what is happening to some degree in many women. Many of us have stepped outside the personal and that amounts to being outside love, well—that is a frightening and dangerous thing to have done. One has to suppose from what one sees about one, knows about others, and is in oneself, that we are impelled to experience the suffering of not having; at the same time that we undergo the discipline of doing our own thinking; and that nothing less than bearing the conflict of these two in one's own nature teaches us who we are in ourselves.

Perhaps this is the road we have to follow, and to thus learn that every sorrow we meet on the way is our sorrow, every mistake we make is something we need to know in order to become oneself. Creating a center within ourselves may be the cultural task that lies ahead. It is yet to do and though it has been begun, even splendidly begun, one cannot say how it is to be continued. It could not be as clear as that, for it is the growth that is taking place within the individual woman, and all that will accrue to society by her increasing integration. The women who already have a center of steadiness in themselves would go no further than to say that it is the place where they have learned, from where they hope to grow, and where an inner relationship exists between their love and their understanding.

It seems to be a conscious and creative remaining at pretty much the place where woman has always been and where life, quite possibly, prefers her to stay. It could be called both a duality and a oneness. It is difficult to know what to call it or how to make it clear, so we still find the feminine quality almost impossible to state.

If further repetition can be borne, further effort to make it a little plainer, then one has to say that woman's true place seems to be the point where opposing things meet, that this uncomfortable, significant, living place is where she makes most sense for others. It is the place where she is not wholly manifest, and so the place where others can see her as they want to see her, and give her all that they need to place in safety. It may be her very lack of definition that is most comforting to others, harmonizing discords in others. It is here that she is restful and useful, just because here the contrasting things lie side by side, but it is her being at this undefined place that also makes her scorned for her nothingness.

In her life comfort and confusion, work and play, solidity and fluidity. She is the bright ideal and the dark shadow, she is the sacred and the unseemly, as well as sacrifice and indulgence. Woman bears the leaden weight of matter, and becomes lost in the mist of not being. She is sense and nonsense, perhaps blindness and wisdom, and such extremes are heavy to carry, particularly heavy when it is uncertain which is a virtue and which is a vice, and worst of all when a quality is both virtue and vice.

If this state of affairs seems too complicated, uncomfortable, and unlikely, it is actually most usual, existing in all of us. If this is doubted let us examine one common characteristic and see if it proves to be simple. Let us look at the quality of vanity which most of us have and which makes us admire ourselves, seek admiration, and also hate ourselves; but which also allows us to enjoy being ourselves. This last happy and innocent state is much more aesthetic in its results than the bleak effects of lacking vanity, or even disliking oneself. For when we are important to ourselves we care whether we behave well or badly. Virtue may become so necessary to us that in order to be thought well of by others we may learn how to make them happy; by loving ourselves we may even learn to love others. So, like most things, vanity is a compound of good and bad, not at all simple, capable of heights and depths; and so it probably is with most of our qualities. When we are harried and pursued by our needs, driven this way and that, then we have to admit that our very unconsciousness can make any quality bad. But if we learn to know them and to hold them loosely, they each flow back and forth as natural as heart beats, now good, now bad.

Because a woman lives so much as a function to others, happy or unhappy in the measure that she is valued by others, always judging herself by being needed, by being loved or noticed or ignored, it becomes part of her very being to need value from others. This is her great weakness, better to say one of her many weaknesses, for a woman has usually lacked achievement by which to measure herself. Man, too, wonders about his own value—is it not the painful point of growth for all?—but man's value is often built for him by others, and it usually rests solidly on work done. The uneasy self-measuring ego that is in everyone, can in man take some rest, and feel some satisfaction in what he has accomplished and in what he knows.

A man can dismiss his worry about his value, and this makes him comfortable to himself and to others, while a woman may have few grounds for satisfaction unless she rests happily in the heart of some one person; or unless from some great simplicity of heart she transcends needs and gives generously; and she does this so frequently that it is hardly noticed. Now her modern accomplishments do help her to rest in herself, and though she may scorn herself as a woman she knows that her work is good, which means that she measures herself with self-respect, but by an odd footrule. It undoubtedly has the new and strange, and good and bad, result that she is less in need of love.

Many women now have specialized interests; at last they have reached a place where they are genuinely interested in a given thing. They are informed and have many ideas and many commitments. This would seem to be a great gain; no longer dependent on others for their value, and with little danger of falling into their own emptiness when life and interest is not offered by others. They are free of the old charge of being so personal that unless one loved them there was nothing to say to them. Now they are strong in the authority of their knowledge, receptive with professional skill, living a full life, and to be envied. They seem complete in themselves, individuals in fact. But by being so defined they have apparently upset proportion, and as women they are often alone. So if individuals are not wanted as wives it is as well that women should note the fact.

But being undefined allows one to be near the sources of life, and then a woman represents to others more than she is in herself. Then she is life to others, not a doctor or a lawyer, but a living person, and it is her simple humanity that makes her rewarding to others. It is as though others reach life through her, which makes the degree of her humanity and goodness matter in some immeasurable way. Perhaps she is and always will be the guardian of the gates of life and death, since if someone comes to her for life and she holds him for herself, then she can be death. They may come to her for value and she may value untruly, making good into bad, or sometimes making bad into good; or they may come to her for love, and love being so near indulgence and abandonment, love brings ruin not life.

She is told by psychologists that she represents the earth, the body, darkness, as man represents light and enlightenment, and thought and spirit. To be the earth and the body is not personal, it is deeper than the personal. If she is these things for others, it is most important to say that to herself she is not wholly these things, only sometimes. The assumption seems to be that she should look at herself through these masculine glasses, but that is the man's view of her, and to herself she is quite different. Her experience of herself is often an experience of lonely awareness, the aloneness increased just because others come to her to find themselves, not to find her. So though she lives participation and oneness, she also knows detachment, a detachment that is very deep.

All these contrasting things are true of woman, and just because she begins to know them consciously and feels a desperate need to integrate them, to take possession of herself to some degree, enough perhaps to make it safe to give herself, she wonders how she can draw a protecting circle about herself within which she may be free to grow.

This is a task of great delicacy, for when the masculine enters the feminine circle as love, or as the spirit, it can be safely received, for then it gives birth to new life or to a new value; but when the masculine enters as idea there is danger of the circle breaking. If the idea is fired with blind zeal a harpy may be present, and the circle will have been destroyed. Woman has mysteries to discover within herself that will not cease to be true just because she ignores them, or because to talk of them at all sounds irrational in this rational age.

It is very frightening, but there are many signs of its truth, that we have now reached a place from where women may evolve our own reality, or from where we may attempt to deny our own depths. We are free to escape into the aggression of our protest at being women, into the kind of thought that splits us, and into a grudging hold on our own egos. Or we may learn to see ourselves and be ourselves even when living for others. We have long needed a goddess to worship and to fear, a goddess who would be all sides of selflessness and of mercy. She would also be the goddess of the body, of love, and of hate as well, for we need to know our own destructiveness; and perhaps it is this vision that must be born in our hearts.

The New Morality

A n d now is it in the least clear what woman is in herself? Would it win agreement to suggest that the masculinity of the modern woman is a living of her latent side because in no other way could she make it hers, or could she prove to herself that it existed? We almost have to believe, since it is happening, that this was the only way in which woman could create herself as an individual. There must always have been women of marked individuality who lived their wholeness naturally, but now a new thing is among us. It is happening all about us, and it amounts to nothing less than women taking on their own individuality. Not living only as a function to others, but standing between their own good and their own bad with a center, a painful and brave center of awareness, where they know they are themselves. They are attempting, and of course failing and also happily succeeding, in the integration of their masculine thought and will, adding these to devoted acceptance. It is perhaps part of the new integration that is taking place in both men and women, a new responsibility for the conflict in the soul of the individual.

Women see very clearly that they have cause for pride and for shame, they realize that being without any awareness of themselves is not at all the same as being selfless. Believe them, for they know, having been both. They no longer wholly believe in the old selflessness that was wanted of them, and society must not ask them to be blind any longer, not for love's sake or for any of the lesser reasons, since it then follows that they are blind about themselves. They begin to feel it would be safer, and they are bravely getting ready to take on the conflict of their paradox.

But because woman's increased consciousness brings her new sorrows and new dangers, and because her new freedom severs her from old anchors to reality, she may be in great danger. When she has contraceptives and economic independence she has stepped outside the old concept of woman, and has only her own trueness and insight to guide her. If women are not to be rooted in their life-giving bodies, what serves them as compass? It needs great understanding to see that what looks like opportunity may also be the place where they leave themselves behind. What they discard may be the part that tended someone whose defenses were down, and who cried out to us from naked need; whom we had to tend because he belonged to us and we belonged to him. We have always been in the muddle of life, putting right for a moment, repairing again and again the thing that would soon go wrong, accepting suffering, accepting being broken, knowing that life was greater than we were, but wanting to be used by it.

Yet one does not choose to be broken, and choice being a new thing for us, we very naturally choose freedom from compulsion. We choose above all to be in possession of ourselves. We choose the borrowed pleasures of interest in the factual, the zest of ideas, and the liberation of theories. These are wine to us after generations of petty detail, personal whim, and forever dealing with vulnerable egos that had to be indulged and lied to.

But woman has held contradiction in her keeping for so long that when she enters the world of organized efficiency she may discover that she has cast away her instinctive self. Then she can easily collapse, since the impersonal world in which the individual is less important than the group can starve her heart. It is constantly said that it is difficult to organize women, their pattern of life not fitting in easily to labor demands. The subject is large, so there is room for a sigh of relief that woman is still unregenerate and still natural. She has always been so close to life that she finds its chaos natural. Its contrasts and its conflicts were often for her to resolve, and the pain of many of them could only be assuaged by her acceptance and her love. This agelong experience is hers, and it means that at some deep place she is tempered and truly strong.

This is the place we have won for ourselves, by endurance and compassion, and it is the place where we have greatness. If we desert it for something made easy by the mind, the loss could be immeasurable. We are immune from much that man has to meet, but he is immune from much that we have known. Men have been a little less helpless than we have been, not caught by life as intimately as we have been, nor as often forced to deal with the dirt of those we love, their physical and their moral dirt. It may be just because we have lived the inferior role that we have a deep experience of the good and bad of life, and we know that they are parts of one whole, measurers of each other. Our knowledge of evil is our strength and we have gained it by having to love those who were evil.

Life has beaten us into reaching a place, or glimpsing a place that is beyond good and evil. It was the only place we could escape to, or perhaps it is truer to say that we drew near to it because we could not escape. We learned truths by living them with our bodies and knowing them in our hearts, by having to accept, and so we have pity for those we bring into life as well as tenderness for those we help out of life.

We have learned so much, and much of it so painfully, that we must not let it go. For very safety we must bind our old way and our new way together. No one can help us but ourselves, but it is almost certain that there is an arrow of direction in us that will enable us to achieve a balance between our warring sides, and allow us to take the past into the future. Our very essence is that of being held in a living experience, of accepting conflict because there is no other way, so it is here our treasure lies.

It may be that woman's long-tested ability to contain opposing things, and her new ability to do it consciously and creatively, is the very essence of the cultural task required of her. Out of necessity and out of tenderness woman has learned to hold good and evil together, since the pain of doing this needs love. It could be nothing less than this that society now asks of her.

The very need of the times and the best quality in woman seem to synchronize, so the task she must apparently undertake gives her her creative possibility. The chances of it being done from her bad side are also there, and the responsibility is enough to daunt any individual woman; yet as there are such evident signs of the feminine principle rising to power of some kind, each woman will take her share, good or bad, in all that lies ahead.

Perhaps women could only take on their own duality in a highly organized society such as the present. Collectivity is now strong enough to allow the individual to accept the inner conflict. The very threat and danger of the age may have brought about this search for integration within the individual, and war and its aftermath has made us so conscious of evil that we are all forced to make ourselves responsible for our own evil. It is now a truism that we are each good and evil, masculine and feminine, collective and individual. This assumption of duality is a great advance in consciousness and in spiritual hardihood; that is, when it is not a belief that we are all alike, all helpless, but all comfortable in our inability to change anything.

The emergent feminine principle shows in a great gamut from the Assumption of the Virgin becoming an Article of Faith in the Catholic Church, down to the simplest woman trying to understand herself. It is truly as though a concept of wholeness were appearing among us, to counterbalance division and destruction, as though everywhere there is a binding together as a need, as a weakness, and as a value. A search for oneness in the individual and so a new integration, a new idea of relationship and so greater unity, a new vision of evil as inherent neighbor of good and so a new morality. This holding together has to be called feminine. It is the oldest and deepest condition arising in new forms, so perhaps a regression and certainly a danger, but it catches us at our source and we live it hardly knowing what we do.

Can we say that it is also the rise of a new morality that is strangely close to woman's eternal role? If it seems unwarranted to suggest that there is a new morality among us, we only have to look about and ask ourselves what it is that we are doing. What is the containment spoken of by politicians, that belief that the best way to deal with apparently incurable bad is to be ready to take action against it, yet to refrain from taking action, and leave every possible loophole for good to enter in? Even modern taxation is based on our present mood of including all, of giving to the weak what was created by the strong, expressing our conviction that weak and strong must draw close together and be as brothers one to another. A technique for self-understanding, such as analytical psychology offers, helps a patient to become responsible for the conflict in his own nature, which then becomes a point of new life, so in the human soul there is also a new balance sought and sometimes found.

In the human heart the new morality seems to be compassion, we could almost call it the morality of inclusion.

It has much of the feminine in its care of the weak, in its dislike of definition, and in its large indulgence; also in its valor of the heart, and it may be the feminine offering to our troubled time.

A NOTE ABOUT THE AUTHOR

FLORIDA SCOTT-MAXWELL was born in Florida in 1883, and attended school in Pittsburgh and New York. After a few years as an actress, she turned to journalism, writing for various newspapers and magazines in New York. On her marriage to a Scotsman in 1910, she went to live in Scotland and later in England, dividing her time between raising a family and writing plays and books. In her early fifties, after study in London and Zurich, she became a Jungian analytical psychologist. She retired from active practice at the age of seventy. Since her retirement she has broadcast frequently on a variety of subjects for the BBC. Mrs. Scott-Maxwell is the mother of four and has six grandchildren.

This book is set in GRANJON a type named in compliment to Robert Granjon, type-cutter and printer—Antwerp, Lyons, Rome, Paris—active from 1523 to 1590. The boldest and most original designer of his time, he was one of the first to practice the trade of type-founder apart from that of printer.

This type face was designed by George W. Jones, who based his drawings upon a type used by Claude Garamond (1510–61) in his beautiful French books, and more closely resembles Garamond's own than do any of the various modern types that bear his name.

The book was composed, printed, and bound by H. Wolff, New York. Paper manufactured by P. H. Glatfelter Company, Spring Grove, Pennsylvania. Designed by Harry Ford.